Hands-On Literacy Coaching

Hands-On Literacy Coaching

Nancy N. Boyles

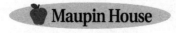

Hands-On Literacy Coaching

Library of Congress Cataloging-in-Publication Data
Boyles, Nancy N., 1948-
    Hands-on literacy coaching / by Nancy N. Boyles.
        p. cm.
    Includes bibliographical references and index.
    ISBN 978-0-929895-53-6 (pbk.)
    1. Language arts teachers—Training of. 2. Language arts. 3.
        Literacy—Study and teaching. I. Title.
LB2844.1.R4B69 2007
372.6044—dc22
                    2007015410

Maupin House publishes professional resources for K-12 educators. Contact us for tailored, in-school training or to schedule an author for a workshop or conference. Visit www.maupinhouse.com for free lesson plan downloads.

Maupin House Publishing, Inc.
2416 NW 71 Place
Gainesville, FL 32653

www.maupinhouse.com
800-524-0634
352-373-5588
352-373-5546 (fax)
info@maupinhouse.com
10 9 8 7 6 5 4 3 2 1

DEDICATION

To my New Haven colleagues:

Imma in Central Office and Trisha and Elaine in the Reading Department—
For your vision and the privilege of being part of that vision.

The Literacy Coaches—
For the passion you bring to your work and for making it so much fun to learn and lead alongside you.

To my graduate students in RDG 662 and RDG 676:

For your tough questions about coaching, endless support, and of course, the chocolate! What would I do on Monday nights without you?

You are the BEST!

TABLE OF CONTENTS

PART II: UNDERSTANDING COACHING

Literacy Instruction and Coaching

Reading Experts "Back in the Day"

When I was an elementary-school student, Miss Lintz, the "remedial reading teacher" in our building, had a little room down a long, dark hallway. I remember going there once or twice to bring her a message and can still picture the tall shelves lined with towering piles of workbooks of the *Dick and Jane* variety (it was that long ago!), plaid phonics skill booklets, and row after row of basal texts. I didn't know what actually *happened* in that room. The only time Miss Lintz appeared in *my* classroom was to collect kids from the "low" reading group, who then presumably disappeared down that dark hallway to engage in...what? I wasn't exactly sure.

Fast forward several decades. Miss Lintz has long since retired and I'm now one of the university faculty members in my state entrusted with the responsibility of preparing literacy leaders to take on Miss Lintz's role in schools—though that role is vastly different from my childhood "remedial reading teacher" image. In our state, we no longer prepare "remedial reading teachers." We prepare "reading specialists" and "reading consultants," though more and more, the real work related to this position is about *literacy coaching*. As a consultant, I also coach both coaches and classroom teachers in their own schools. Much of this work is in an urban district. I often make as many as ten school visits per week, so I see the issues from multiple perspectives.

What is a Literacy Coach?

What is a literacy coach? As in days gone by, the literacy coach at any grade level (K-12) is the resident "reading expert." But unlike the job description under which Miss Lintz probably worked, the field has expanded and now includes both reading and writing (literacy). Perhaps even more significant is that working with struggling readers as Miss Lintz did all day, every day, is only one part—and in fact a diminishing part—of the current literacy coach's role. Today, literacy coaches spend a large percentage of their time working with teachers rather than students.

When you think about it, it makes sense. If the school's reading expert works intensively with a couple of dozen struggling readers, that's great for those twenty-four kids. But when the reading person works with the two dozen teachers in the building, hundreds of students benefit. And so, it's become the responsibility of today's reading specialist or consultant to "coach" her (or his) peers toward a higher level of proficiency in literacy instruction.

This is tricky. First, the literacy coach is not an administrator with the authority to evaluate. That's the job of the principal or assistant principal. The literacy coach needs to be perceived as a support, as an ally, as a peer with the capacity to make you look good as a teacher—as painlessly as possible, some would argue. Succeeding in this role is dependent on two main areas of expertise: understanding literacy instruction and understanding the process of coaching.

Some newly appointed coaches come to their role with a whole graduate program in literacy behind them that has prepared them to tackle head on the challenges of literacy coaching in their school. But what about people who have been reading specialists or consultants for years, whose jobs have sort of morphed into this new set of responsibilities—with no opportunity to learn the skills that this changed role requires? What about teachers who have been plucked from their classrooms and tossed into a coach's position because their district is so eager to move forward with this research-supported notion that in-school coaching enhances students' performance?

The literacy coach needs to be perceived as a support, as an ally, as a peer with the capacity to make you look good as a teacher—as painlessly as possible, some would argue.

"Ms. Simpson is an incredible first-grade teacher. Her students always make wonderful progress in reading," the principal reasons. "We want her to work with all of our primary teachers." The problem is that Ms. Simpson hasn't had a course in reading since she received her undergraduate degree ten years ago. She may be excellent with six-year-olds, but she's never worked with adults. Ms. Simpson (with good reason) feels overwhelmed, bewildered, frustrated, and has no idea where or how to begin. To make matters worse, students' scores on the state literacy assessment have been declining in this school for two years. There's a sense of urgency about fixing what's broken NOW. So where do you start? How do you lead teachers toward excellence in literacy instruction so students can become the best they can be?

What Does a Literacy Coach Do?

What exactly does a literacy coach do? If you asked ten coaches this question, you'd get ten different answers—everything from facilitating professional study groups to implementing projects that link families with the school, to setting up sessions for looking at student work. One response would probably recur, however, as central to the role of *all* coaches: Coaches can be especially helpful right in the classroom, providing sustained support to the teacher over time—recognizing the strengths and needs of individual teachers, modeling best practices, and providing support until teachers become competent and confident with best literacy practices themselves. In short, the greatest responsibility of a coach is to be a teacher of teachers. We need coaches who can support teachers in the same way we want teachers to support kids: through the gradual release of responsibility until they achieve independence. That is, we need coaches who understand explicit literacy instruction.

That, it seems, is the essence of the problem. We hear a lot about explicit literacy instruction through the No Child Left Behind Act (2001). In fact, schools that receive funds from Reading First grants have to prove that the literacy curriculum they use provides "systematic, explicit instruction." Explicit instruction is all the "buzz." But still, most teachers would have a hard time defining it.

The best way to really increase coaches' expertise in supporting teachers is to provide them with a more thorough understanding of what explicit teaching is and how it looks when applied to literacy instruction.

Explicit Instruction: Beyond the Buzz Words

There's an entire journey between the time when a teacher first explains a new concept, to the moment at which students own and use that concept by themselves. Your role as instructional coach is to actively help teachers understand that good instruction is the beginning of the learning process; student independence is the end result. The vehicle that gets them there is explicit teaching with a gradual release of responsibility.

Who's in charge of the task changes gradually throughout the teaching-learning process. The first, *I do, you watch* phase is the kind of teaching that we sometimes call *direct instruction*, where the teacher stands before the whole class or gathers everyone together in a designated area of the room and does most of the talking.

As the teacher transitions from modeling to practicing, everyone may still be sitting together on the rug, but now the responsibility shifts a bit to *I do, you help*. After enough input is elicited from students to know that they can handle more of the responsibility on their own, students may then move back to their own seats or go to tables for small-group guided follow-up.

At this point, we can define the process as *you do, I help*. It is during this phase that instruction needs to be differentiated. Some quick learners will require only one or two passes to attain the desired level of competence, while average achievers will need several attempts. And students who struggle will need even more reinforcement. Teachers may vary the process, the product, or the content. But in the end, all students need to reach the same goal: independence from teacher scaffolding. At last the teaching/learning relationship has become *you do, I watch*. It is not until students reach this level of mastery that we can expect them to do well on a state achievement test, a classroom assessment, or even on a homework assignment.

The steps of explicit instruction fit well within the three formats in which teachers deliver literacy instruction: shared, guided, and independent reading. Teachers explain and model and begin the

Teachers may vary the process, the product, or the content. But in the end, all students need to reach the same goal: independence from teacher scaffolding.

transition to more active student involvement during shared reading (synonymous here with whole-class instruction). Practicing takes place during guided (or small-group) instruction. And independence is achieved through independent (or individualized) reading and writing.

The following chart illustrates this explicit teaching model as applied to comprehensive literacy.

Model of Explicit Instruction (Gradual Release of Responsibility)		
Explain	Shared Reading	I do, you watch
↓	↓	↓
Model		
↓	↓	↓
Bridge		I do, you help
↓	↓	↓
Practice	Guided Reading	You do, I help
↓	↓	↓
Independence	Independent Reading	You do, I watch

This chart begins to create a mental picture of what explicit instruction looks like in the context of comprehensive literacy, but it still does not tell us exactly what we should see happening in the classroom. What should teachers do during shared, guided, and independent reading to lead students toward independence? How will coaches recognize when those things are done well? How can coaches help teachers address and adjust their instruction for optimal student learning?

To answer these questions, I think it's helpful to further refine the components of explicit instruction, organizing them into three broad, sequential phases and then breaking each phase into smaller pieces. There are nine steps in all.

PHASE I. SETTING THE STAGE FOR LITERACY LEARNING

Getting students to care
Activating/building background knowledge
Identifying objectives

PHASE II. BUILDING LITERACY KNOWLEDGE

Explaining
Modeling
Bridging

Guided practice
Independent practice
Reflection

Good instruction is always situated within a context, so this book will also describe elements of the classroom environment and classroom management that contribute to effective, efficient literacy teaching and learning.

What Will You Find in This Book?

To support the notion that literacy coaching has two important components, literacy and coaching, this book will answer two important questions for coaches:

1. What do I need to understand about *literacy instruction* in order to recognize, and help teachers see for themselves, when their literacy teaching is going well—or not so well?

2. What do I need to understand about the *process of coaching* in order to move teachers toward independence in their own implementation of best literacy practices?

Part I: Understanding Literacy Instruction is about the *what* of literacy coaching, identifying what to look for within the three phases of explicit instruction described above, as well as elements of the classroom environment and classroom management.

Chapter One, The Literacy Context: Classroom Environment and Classroom Management, provides a snapshot of classrooms where literacy learners thrive. Several indicators you'll want to see in the environment are described here with examples from classrooms a lot like those that every educator has encountered somewhere along the way. In what ways does the physical set-up of the classroom work for or against optimal literacy learning? Within this context, how do the teacher's management strategies impact students' reading and writing?

Chapter Two addresses the beginning phase of the instructional sequence: Setting the Stage for Literacy Learning. Beyond the design of the room itself, there's the design of the lesson. This chapter looks at what teachers need to do *first*: How can teachers get students to care? How can they get students ready for the reading ahead? How can they identify and clarify a worthy lesson objective? All of these questions are answered in Chapter Two.

Chapter Three is about Building Literacy Knowledge. Teachers explain things to students on a regular basis. But how do you explain something *well*? And then, how do you model your thinking so students can see how a good reader approaches the task, so they can become strategic? Was your modeling effective? How will you know? How will you begin to get students to take ownership of the task? Find the answers to these questions in Chapter Three.

Chapter Four focuses on best practices in Reinforcing Literacy Knowledge. How do we guide students toward independence in reading and writing? How can we help children apply what they know independently in a manner that provides them with both choice and accountability? And finally, how do we get readers, even young readers, to reflect on their learning process so that they may become self-directed readers and writers? Chapter Four provides insights into these important questions.

Part II: Understanding Coaching is about the *how* of coaching and addresses a number of issues that coaches face as they engage in the process of literacy coaching.

Chapter Five, When and How to Intervene, looks at some of the most common problems teachers experience when teaching reading and writing and suggests possible coaching interventions to solve these problems. This chapter divides interventions into two categories— those that can be resolved through discussion and conferring with teachers, and those that are handled most effectively through direct work in the classroom.

Chapter Six, The Coach/Teacher Dynamic, examines interpersonal aspects of coaching. What strengths do you bring to your role as a coach? What about the teachers with whom you work day to day? Where is each one coming from as an adult learner with unique attitudes and dispositions? Chapter Six will provide some insights into these matters of teacher-coach connections and help you understand how different teachers need different kinds of coaching support.

Chapter Seven, Principles and Protocols of Effective Literacy Coaching, answers a number of questions that are on every coach's mind—among them: *Who should get coached?* and *How many teachers should I coach at one time?* The chapter concludes with several coaching protocols along with a description of how each form can be used by coaches to support a specific coaching need.

Chapter Eight, Applying What You Know, provides three teaching scenarios for coaches to analyze through vicarious visits to classrooms where literacy instruction is underway. Use all you have learned in this book to identify each teacher's strengths, instructional needs, and next coaching steps. These scenarios are especially effective for professional development sessions in which literacy coaches come together to refine their practice.

Visit: www.maupinhouse.com/boylesanalyses.php for an analysis of the strengths and weaknesses of each of the teaching scenarios in this chapter and to submit your own analysis to me (Nancy Boyles) for possible publication on the website.

How Can This Book Be Used for Professional Development?

When I introduce the content of this book in my graduate classes or in workshops or institutes that I conduct, it takes me about five hours to present the material contained in Part I and five hours to present the material in Part II. Of course this does not always occur in a single session. Individual chapters can be addressed in shorter periods of time, depending on what your schedule will allow.

Coaches may want to first meet together to consider points relevant to each chapter and to decide how to best use the information to guide their coaching. They may also want to determine a means of sharing the information with administrators and teachers.

Study questions are included at the end of each chapter to guide your professional conversations and to alert you to some of the points made in the chapter that you won't want to miss.

Who Will Benefit from This Book?

The audience that will benefit most centrally from this book will be literacy coaches. They may be called "consultants" or "specialists" or "mentors." They may be External or Internal Literacy Facilitators supplied through a Reading First grant. But whatever their title, and however they arrived at your schoolhouse door, they are the school-based literacy leader who works with both students and teachers. In fact, maybe this person works only with teachers. If you are this individual, this book is for you.

I hope this book can also support administrators. Not every principal comes to her or his administrative role with a background in literacy. How well do you really understand what you're looking at when you visit a classroom to observe a literacy lesson? All of the kids seem happy and busy, and the teacher is following the core program manual, but why are reading test scores from this classroom always so low? The principal's (or the curriculum director's) interest in this book will not be quite the same as the coach's; it won't be her job to actually solve the teacher's problem. However, if she can help to identify what needs strengthening, she and the coach can work together to help the classroom teacher.

The audience I'd be most happy to serve with this book is classroom teachers themselves. Let's be realistic: Even the most organized, most efficient literacy coach won't be able to devote himself to any one teacher in a school for endless periods of time. The best way for teachers to move from good to great in their pursuit of instructional excellence is for them to become self-reflective practitioners with a clear understanding of what they're doing, and why they're doing it. This book can get all teachers closer to that goal.

When I share the information contained in this book with students in my graduate classes, invariably someone will raise her hand and say, "I wish I knew all of this about explicit instruction when I was preparing my induction year portfolio. I could have done a much better job."

I, too, wish that all teachers entered the profession with a solid grasp of explicit literacy instruction and how to best implement it in their classrooms. But until that happens, I hope the chapters that follow will provide both a vision of instructional excellence and a means of getting there.

The journey begins in the chapter that follows, right in the classroom, with a careful look at the classroom environment and classroom management.

Part I
Understanding
Literacy Instruction

1

The Literacy Context: Classroom Environment and Classroom Management

The First Classroom Visit

Sometimes it is helpful to visit a classroom initially when it is not literacy time. That way, you can take in all that the walls and the space have to offer and get a sense of the general classroom environment without the burden of needing to learn all you can right away about the teacher's literacy instruction. And similarly, when you come back to see the teacher and students engaged in literacy, you won't be side-tracked by that incredible data wall or alluring library corner that you are seeing for the first time.

Your initial coaching visit should be a bit more than a "three-minute classroom walk-through," as it is commonly defined. This first visit may take more like seven to ten minutes and is only one component of a more complete classroom analysis that includes a thorough examination of literacy instruction. Although administrators can use it to evaluate teachers, this model is aimed first and foremost at coaches who want to help teachers reflect on and improve their instructional practices in the teaching of reading and writing. And teachers themselves can use it for self-reflection, too.

Begin with Eyes Wide Open

To begin coaching, you don't really need to *do* anything; you just need to *look*. Today's classroom is its own mini-world with a unique culture different from any other—across the state or even across the hall. Where to focus first? What should we look for? What do we hope to see? And how will we know whether what we see contributes to creating a place where literacy learners thrive?

In order to answer these questions, we need two points of focus—the classroom environment and the classroom management—as both contribute to the context in which the literacy learning takes place.

Looking into the Classroom Environment

Admittedly, first impressions can be very subjective and may not be predictive of what the environment or management is like every day of the year. Still, it is a place to begin. While it may be relatively easy for us to agree on those classrooms that look and feel especially inviting and practically "run themselves," or those rooms that are really depressing or chaotic, between those two extremes personal preferences play a large role in that first, overall impression.

In the first part of this chapter we will examine factors related to the classroom environment—those that support literacy teaching and learning and those that undermine it. The end of the chapter will focus on general aspects of classroom management that impact students' reading and writing.

WHAT IS THE CLASSROOM DÉCOR?

I am particularly sensitive to what I perceive as visual overload. There is so much "stuff" in some rooms that you don't know where to look first. I vividly remember one room in a school where I was coaching coaches. I walked into a big-as-life tropical hut sporting a huge straw-topped umbrella that could have kept the sun off of at least eight large adults. Just a few steps later, I walked through a wooden gate (same classroom) to another space decorated in the image of a city park with benches, a live tree, and assorted flowering shrubs. There may also have been children in the room somewhere. We found them after the principal had a little "chat" with the teacher.

My point is that I think we sometimes go a little overboard in the decorating department. Too much and the décor turns into clutter, whether it's "attractive" clutter as described above, or the more traditional clutter found in the room of the teacher who hasn't thrown out a piece of paper or a paper clip in decades.

Room spaces and classroom materials should support the literacy work we want our children to do—not dominate it. Teetering piles of papers that children knock against are obviously in the way. But sometimes, that comfortable beanbag chair can be, too. Or, the little lamp that may light up a dark library corner but falls over at least twice each day as kids pass by swinging their book bags.

Classrooms can be fun and functional without looking like your living room. The important point your first impression raises is: What does the teacher do with what's in her room? You might ask: How do you use the beanbag chair? What purpose does that little lamp serve? If the teacher doesn't know, maybe the space or the "stuff" could be cleaned out or eliminated.

HOW IS THE ROOM ARRANGED?

Once beyond the initial "Wow!" or "Oh, no!" you can begin to look at how the teacher uses the space to support literacy instruction. Are the desks in clusters inviting conversation and collaboration (or can they be easily configured that way when needed), or is each student destined to remain a small island in a sea of desks dotting the classroom? Are there clearly defined areas for the whole class to work together, tables where small groups of children may gather with or without the teacher, as well as spaces to curl up individually with a good book?

Classrooms without tables or a space available for small groups to work hint that little time may be devoted to small-group reading instruction in this room. Without a place for the whole class to congregate, I wonder about the classroom's sense of community. Do students spend the entire day tethered to their desks?

I'm also curious about the placement of the teacher's desk: Is it center stage or off to the side, like a prop that supports the classroom cast? And what about traffic flow? Can you get from that little boy flagging you down in the back left-hand corner to the young gentleman in front by the window who seems more engaged in the game on the playground than in his reading assignment?

ASK THE TEACHER:
- Where do you work with small groups of students?
- Where do students read independently?
- Where do they work on projects?
- Where do they sit when you're teaching a shared (whole-class) reading lesson?

HOW IS STUDENT WORK DISPLAYED?

Next I note the student work displayed on walls and bulletin boards. Of course we want the work to be current, not something that's old, faded, and torn. But just being fresh and new is not a high enough standard. What kind of thinking does the work represent? Do the products demonstrate that students have been thinking critically and creatively, or are they 25 identical, fill-in-the-blank worksheets? Differentiated instruction should yield differentiated products.

Look beyond cute and colorful. The fun bulletin board that catches your eye may be more a tribute to students' art skills than their literacy development. Does the teacher actually refer to those charts for choosing "just right" books from the classroom library for instructional purposes, or do they simply fill a space?

Similarly, we should be wary of those nifty teacher-store cardboard cut-outs of grammar rules, tips about narrative writing, and other dos and don'ts of reading and writing. These posters often sport cartoon characters of different ethnicities, a fairly superficial way of honoring student diversity. Instead, look for evidence of real respect for diversity in the classroom, such as books that feature children from different cultures, or the presence of parents and other adults from various places around the globe who contribute to the classroom, sharing their traditions and supporting students.

ASK THE TEACHER:
- Which displays are tied to grade-level objectives?
- How do you make sure that *all* children have work displayed on a regular basis?

HOW VISIBLE ARE THE LEARNING OBJECTIVES?

Teachers who teach to clear objectives and provide sharply focused instruction have no trouble defining the objective that accompanies their lesson. Posting the objective next to the products that measure student success with a lesson is a way for everyone who passes by to see not just *what* students did but *why*. What was the reason for the assignment? Where was the teacher going with this? When teachers title their display "Our Stories about Winter" or "Book Reports about Famous Americans" or "Our Best Work," there is no indication of what the students were striving to achieve in their winter stories or book reports or what makes this work their "best."

ASK THE TEACHER:
- What counted as "success" for this task?
- What kind of written feedback do you think is *most* helpful to students?

WHAT KIND OF WRITTEN FEEDBACK TO PROVIDE TO STUDENTS?

Be sure to take note of teachers' comments on the student work that hangs around the room. Useful feedback to students on written assignments is honest, constructive, and specific. Kids know when their work is praiseworthy, so praising the sub-standard stuff quickly diminishes a teacher's credibility; soon students won't believe the comments even when the sentiment is genuine.

The biggest mistake I see teachers make with their written feedback revolves around the generality of their comments: "Good work," "Nice effort," "Needs more details." So what's *good* about the work or noteworthy about the *effort*? And as for the *details*, if the student knew where to insert more details, or what kind of details to add, he probably would have put them there in the first place.

Look for specific comments that help the student improve next time, like "Good use of quotation marks in this piece," or "Your title page shows lots of care and creativity," or "Consider adding some more physical details in paragraph three about what your character *looks like* so I can picture her better."

ASK THE TEACHER:
• What made this a "good job," an "A"?
• How will this student know what to do to achieve similar success next time—or improve to be more successful?

ARE RUBRICS USED AS AN INSTRUCTIONAL TOOL?

Offering useful feedback is easier when teachers use rubrics that identify the criteria by which a student is evaluated. Rubrics make the grading process transparent and much fairer to students. (Remember all those papers we got back from teachers when we were students with the "A-" or "C+," or whatever the grade was, plunked at the bottom of the final page? We had no clue much of the time about what made that paper an "A-" rather than an "A.")

But rubrics only help if students can *see* them. They need to be visible. Students need to be able to refer to them so they can check their performance against the established criteria. That means *we* should be able to see them too as *we* look around the room. Some teachers post classroom rubrics in chart form, using different rubrics for different literacy components: expository writing, application of comprehension strategies, reading fluency. In other classrooms, the rubrics may be part of a student's reading or writing folder.

In *all* classrooms, you should be able to "catch" students referring to their rubrics.

They also need to be simple and easy for the student to understand. A visible rubric written in overly sophisticated language is of as little use as no rubric at all. An example from an inappropriate rubric related to critical thinking, for example, might require of a second grader: "Synthesize relevant information from within a written work to write a personal response to the text." Show me the eight-year-old who can interpret that! In *all* classrooms, you should be able to "catch" students referring to their rubrics. It's this active use of rubrics you'll hope to observe as you look around a classroom the first time.

Note that on a return visit, you might want to probe more deeply because with rubrics, there's much more than meets the eye. On one level, a rubric helps the teacher by breaking a task into its component parts so that student performance can be measured more accurately and reliably. That's a good start. Used well, however, rubrics can also lead to more focused instruction by isolating points of weakness that can be addressed specifically. As a teacher thumbs through her stack of rubrics related to today's written response to comprehension questions, you hope she takes note of that one child who still doesn't understand topic sentences. You hope she makes a mental note to confer with this child individually. You hope that the teacher red-flags the six students who are having trouble finding more than one detail to support a main point and thinks: *Okay, I'll meet with these six students as a group tomorrow.* You hope the teacher ponders: *What's this? No one is using quotation marks correctly? It looks like we'll need a whole-class lesson on that topic.*

ASK THE TEACHER:

• How do you use rubrics to help students reflect on the quality of their work?

• How could you express criteria on your rubric in language that [second graders] can comprehend?

• What do you do with the information you obtain from your rubrics?

IS STUDENT DATA MEASURED AND DISPLAYED FOR MOTIVATION?

With the emphasis on scientifically based reading research (SBRR) to inform instruction, it is no surprise that specific feedback and carefully constructed rubrics are not enough. There is a huge push toward accountability in literacy education (as we all know from our state assessment tests.) How do teachers know that students are making progress? What's the evidence? What kind of data validates a teacher's claims? Prove it!

Good classrooms have become laboratories of well-defined reading and writing initiatives where student performance is measured systematically over time. There are charts describing the results of these initiatives taped to chalk boards and hanging outside of classrooms. Such charts do not single out individual students in a punitive way, but rather, provide a "status check" for the class in general. Some are roughly drawn bar graphs that six-year-olds have colored with fat crayons. Others are fancy, computer-generated pie charts designed by fourth graders that I couldn't create if my life depended on it. "Number of First Graders in Room 15 Who Reached Goal on Sight Words: October, December, February, April, June," proclaims one data wall hanging outside a classroom I visit often. Students see for themselves the progress they are making. Parents can see it. Everyone passing that classroom can see it.

In other classrooms, teachers look confused when you mention data. "Data? What data?" There is no evidence of data charted and posted anywhere. Some teachers pay little attention to the power of such visual displays to motivate students and provide public testimony to teaching and learning.

ASK THE TEACHER:

• What kind of data do you have that you could display to motivate students to strive for their "personal best?"

• How can you make your data wall interactive so students really *use* the information it provides?

ARE WORD WALLS USED EFFECTIVELY?

Word walls have become a staple of primary classrooms. Typically they contain high-frequency words that young children find helpful for both reading and writing, or words that relate to a curriculum theme. In classrooms where these are used effectively, the words change periodically and the word wall is a high-utility classroom resource: "When you need a word for your writing piece on baby animals," the second-grade teacher reminds her class, "be sure to check the word wall before checking with me." You will see even little first graders scan a word wall for a word that they *know* is there so they can use it in their story. They can find their word because there are a reasonable number of words stapled to the board, and they are organized, perhaps in alphabetical order. And they are written large enough to be seen from across the room!

I love it when I also see word walls in classrooms beyond the primary level. This is a great way to keep kids focused on vocabulary that supports their writing. Some examples: "Words to Use Instead of 'Said'"; "Strong Verbs"; words that connect to social studies and science themes: "Weather Words" and "Words from the Wild West"; or words related to a piece of literature students are studying: "Wonderful Words from *Charlotte's Web*" and "Wicked Words from *The Witches*." In both primary and upper-grade classrooms, word walls used well are like a lifeline to students as they learn to use new words for listening, speaking, reading, and writing.

> In both primary and upper-grade classrooms, word walls used well are like a lifeline to students as they learn to use new words for listening, speaking, reading, and writing.

Compare this to classrooms where word walls serve mostly as wallpaper. Curious about the beautiful word wall I saw displayed in one second-grade classroom, I asked one of the students to tell me about it. "I don't know," he shrugged. "My teacher didn't tell us yet; she just put the words up this morning right before you came."

Some teachers are very good at "talking the talk," and unfortunately, in some cases, this is enough to allow them to slide through. When you gaze upon that word wall, you do not want to see hundreds of words swimming before your eyes. You do not want to see words written in such small print that students need to squint to read them. You do not want to see them curled and faded, as if they have been stapled to that same square-inch of space since the teacher's first day on the job long ago.

ASK THE TEACHER:
• What's the purpose behind that great-looking word wall—and how do students use it?
• What other kinds of word walls or charts would be helpful to your students?

ARE BOOKS AN INTEGRAL PART OF THE CLASSROOM?

When I enter some classrooms, I want to unpack my bags and live there. It's about the books! I have an almost insatiable love for (addiction to?) children's books and, in some rooms, there are so many books—both old favorites and books new to me—that I just want to grab one off the shelf and curl up with it in a cozy corner. *What's that new picture book hidden behind the big stuffed bear? Wow, I never saw this book of fables before! What a beautiful photo journal about life in a pond, perfect for young readers who delight in nonfiction.* Books, books, books of so many genres beckoning to me. Surely life can't get better than this!

Other classrooms are nearly devoid of books or other print sources for students to read independently. When asked about this, some teachers reply (rather indignantly) that they keep *asking* for books at their school, but there's no money in the school budget to purchase any. While this may be true, there are so many free or inexpensive ways of acquiring children's books that this excuse hardly seems justified. Garage sales are one source. Parents are often looking for loving homes for books their children have outgrown. With a little effort and ingenuity, it's not difficult to stock a classroom with suitable reading material.

Still other classrooms have books but don't value them. They're stuffed willy-nilly into bookcases—some beyond the easy reach of students—or piled randomly on counters with no system of leveling them or sorting them by genre. Students can't see what's available or dislodge a selection without setting off an avalanche that sends the remaining books crashing to the floor. This is not a scenario that encourages reading!

ASK THE TEACHER:

- What have you done to acquire free or inexpensive books or other print resources for your classroom that cover a variety of genres?
- What kind of system could you use to level and arrange your books that would provide easy access to the materials and entice students to read?
- How can you keep your books organized for continued ease of use?

IS TECHNOLOGY USED TO SUPPORT LITERACY?

Notice that I placed my discussion of books before this section on technology because I'm less impressed by technology than the way it's used. It's hard *not* to be dazzled by the array of technology that greets you in some of the fabulous, brand-new schools I've had the opportunity to visit. Banks of computers, document cameras, smart boards, video and DVD players, distance-learning networks, LCD projectors, and a host of other techno-phenomena of which I barely know the names are transforming literacy instruction, along with software programs that support early reading and struggling readers and writers with special needs. Some teachers and students use all of this seamlessly—and that's the key.

As you look around the classroom, how does the technology seem to be integrated into the curriculum? Do these kindergarten students know how to get themselves onto the computer independently for their daily reading-practice session? Does this fourth-grade teacher understand how to take advantage of the document camera for turning an excerpt of text into a shared reading lesson?

ASK THE TEACHER:

- What technology do you have in this room and how do you use it?
- What additional technology would you like to have available to you? How would it support student learning?

HOW ARE LEARNING CENTERS AND WORKSTATIONS FUNCTIONING?

If we want students to get better at reading and writing, they need to read and write. Classroom time that is not devoted to direct instruction should be spent at authentic, independent tasks with sufficient accountability to reinforce students' reading and writing skills and strategies. In the past decade, centers—and more lately, workstations—have been touted as the way to provide students with those authentic experiences.

But their presence or absence is not necessarily, in my view, a good thing or a bad thing—until we take a deeper look. Whether authentic literacy practice can happen best at a special place in the classroom other than the student's desk is for each teacher to decide. What is not acceptable, however, is that some centers/workstations function as a new setting for busy work—providing ditto-sheet-quality activities with no integral connection to the curriculum but which keep kids occupied while the teacher meets with small guided-reading groups. The only difference between busy work from "back in the day" and the activities found in some centers or workstations is that students now walk to their work sheet rather than having it delivered to their desk.

ASK THE TEACHER:

- How are your workstation/center activities connected to your curriculum?
- How do you differentiate these activities based on students' literacy needs?

ARE STUDENTS ENCOURAGED TO SELF-REFLECT?

In classrooms of all levels, I am especially gratified when I see students' written reflections on their reading and writing processes. This might be a sentence strip penned by a third grader who proclaims, "I figured out a word to describe the main character in my book by noticing what she said and what she was thinking in her mind." It could be a fifth grader's description of how he goes about revising a piece of writing to include "snapshots."

Self-reflection on literacy performance still is more the exception than the norm, but it is a powerful indicator of the rigor of the teaching and the value placed on reflection in that classroom. It also demonstrates the vital metacognitive component—that students are actively engaged in thinking about their thinking, and that thinking in this classroom is here to stay!

Of course, in your initial classroom visit, you'll want to be as unobtrusive as possible. But, if you are peeking over a little shoulder and just can't pass up the opportunity to get a bit more insight into the student's concept of himself as a learner, I offer some advice a professor once shared with me way back at the beginning of my teaching career.

ASK THE STUDENT:

• What are you doing?
• Why are you doing it?
• What will you do tomorrow?

If a student can articulate a thoughtful response to these three questions, you can feel good that this is a classroom where the learning process is celebrated on an ongoing basis.

How Coaches Can Support Teachers in Enhancing the Classroom Environment

A principal that I know and like very much decided she just couldn't stand the appearance of one of her teacher's classrooms any longer. She had spoken with the teacher on many occasions and encouraged her to do a little sprucing up—but to no avail. So, with the best of intentions, she and her literacy coach spent several hours one Friday evening cleaning out and rearranging. The room looked considerably better come Monday morning, but the teachers' union was not favorably impressed. So, what can coaches do to provide truly helpful help? **Chapter Five** describes coaching interventions in many areas of literacy, including suggestions for enhancing the classroom environment.

A checklist to analyze the classroom environment is provided along with other coaching protocols in **Chapter Seven**. The items on this checklist are things you hope to see in most classrooms. If your school promotes additional or different features in its classrooms, simply modify the checklist accordingly. As suggested above, this checklist may be used by the classroom teacher for self-reflection, by the school administrator for evaluation, or by the literacy coach as a source of discussion about features of the classroom environment that contribute to students' literacy learning. Coaches should definitely not use the rating scale; that is provided for administrators' use only. Or perhaps the classroom teacher would like to self-score as a means of deciding on priority areas for her own professional growth.

A word about the rating scale: I consider a rating of "2" to be a good score. This denotes competence. The feature may not be perfect, but the teacher clearly has the right idea and it is consistently present. Reserve a "3" score for the real stand-outs, for situations so good that you can't wait for other teachers in your school to come in and witness it for themselves, or for the local TV station to send a features crew in. That's a "3." Use this same mindset in thinking about teachers' performance in the section that follows on classroom management, and in later chapters, too.

Classroom Management

ARE CLEAR ROUTINES FOR CLASSROOM PROCEDURES IN PLACE?

Good classroom management makes teaching look almost effortless. In fact, the classroom pretty much seems to run itself. But nothing could be farther from the truth! That even, steady rhythm of kids flowing from one area of the room to another, from the first activity to the next, is the work of a teacher who has invested much effort to craft classroom routines. When you enter one of these well-managed classrooms where students are self-directed and go about their work with both purpose and passion, it is easy to focus on the literacy instruction that is taking place.

In other classrooms, teachers' instruction is punctuated by constant— and I mean *constant*—interruptions from students who don't seem to know what to do next: "Louis, why are you out of your seat? Sit down!" "What do you mean, you don't know how to do this page? I *told* you how to do this page." "No, you can't go to the office right this minute to see if your mother dropped off your lunch." The verbal exchange is endless. During one small group lesson I watched, the teacher stopped her teaching twelve times within a fifteen-minute period to deal with things that had nothing to do with her small-group lesson.

"I *wish* my class could work independently," decry many teachers. They say this as if again this year they've been "stuck" with all of the kids in their grade who can't work without constant supervision, like all the great workers mysteriously got assigned to the teacher across the hall. Little by little, independent work habits need to be taught so managing our students does not undermine the time we should be spending teaching our students. It is nearly impossible for the coach (or even the teacher) to work on literacy until classroom routines have been established.

ARE CLEAR EXPECTATIONS FOR STUDENT BEHAVIOR IN PLACE?

Like classroom routines, expectations for student behavior are also a prerequisite for productive teaching. Sometimes I enter a classroom to conduct a model lesson and the unstated, though implied, message from the teacher is, "Teach this lesson on making inferences (or whatever) ...and while you're at it, see what you can do about fixing the behavior of those six kids at the back table."

What the teacher is really asking me to do is, in the space of an hour, get behaviors back on track that she has neglected for three months, since the beginning of the school year. This is an unrealistic assignment for any coach.

To some extent, a well-crafted lesson will engage students and some of those negative behaviors will disappear on their own. But students who have become accustomed to responding rudely, tuning out instruction, or distracting the student at the next desk will not necessarily be reformed by one good lesson by the literacy coach. Teachers need to get behaviors in hand *before* calling upon the service of their literacy coach if they want the focus to be on literacy.

Teachers need to get behaviors in hand *before* calling upon the service of their literacy coach if they want the focus to be on literacy.

IS THE PACING AND ORCHESTRATION OF INSTRUCTION APPROPRIATELY INTENSE?

When I visit some classrooms to see what's going on, I leave tired but satisfied at the end of the morning. It's a healthy kind of tired, that feeling that you've done a good day's work and have lots to show for your efforts. Technically, I haven't even done the work; the kids have done it, and all I've had to do is keep pace.

The best classrooms have a steady, quick rhythm with almost no down time. Teacher and students stay focused on the learning goal with all actions directed toward a clearly defined outcome. The teacher sets the tone and the agenda and children quickly realize that they are expected to hold up their end of the bargain in getting their work done—on time!

Some teachers confuse a healthy pace with warp speed and a sort of frenzy emerges that leaves both teachers and students discouraged, like they can never quite catch up or measure up. When the routine is too ambitious with too much crammed into it, even the most conscientious effort ends in frustration and a feeling of inadequacy.

In other classrooms, the pace is too slow. The teacher's goals set forth in the lesson plan are modest at best. Children make a game of diverting the teacher's attention from the instructional focus with a well-calculated question or distracting behavior. In these classrooms, teachers often tell me with a sigh, "No time for small-group instruction again today." They see themselves as victims of a crowded curriculum rather than masters of their own destiny.

IS THE TEACHING RIGOROUS WITH HIGH EXPECTATIONS?

But efficiency isn't the only indicator of instructional intensity. An equally important contributor is rigor. Rigor is a much-heralded term lately that is used—and abused—to signify that important work is happening in a classroom. I chuckled to myself recently when I heard a teacher compliment her class for how well they were "sitting with rigor."

Beyond the obvious misuses of the word, what does rigor entail? Rigorous teaching and learning are characterized by curriculum and instruction of breadth and depth, where expectations are high for *all* students. It is small-group instruction that is targeted to students' specific needs—not just time set aside to work with a few children around the kidney-shaped table in the corner of the classroom for the sake of appearances when the principal comes to visit. It is comprehension strategy instruction that is systematic and explicit with a clear lesson objective, not just repeated modeling of a single strategy by the teacher. It is differentiated instruction with opportunities for inquiry and instructional processes matched to students' learning styles, not different students doing different worksheets. Indeed, intense teaching is rigorous teaching.

IS MORE TIME SPENT ON ACADEMICS THAN NON-ACADEMICS?

The issue here is that students sometimes spend more time drawing about their reading and writing than they spend reading and writing.

Something else that sabotages literacy and other academics in some classrooms is art. I am a huge supporter of the arts in education and, in fact, think we could be doing much more to integrate both graphic and performing arts into our curriculum. But that's not the issue here. The issue here is that students sometimes spend more time drawing about their reading and writing than they spend reading and writing.

My best example of this is a personal one. My daughter was one of those kids who loved to draw. I remember a story she wrote way back in the primary grades about a Sunday afternoon we spent as a family at the county fair. The story was a short one with a sentence about each of several events we enjoyed that day. The book she created of this story contained a single sentence per page and a picture. She probably drafted the sentences in a total of twenty minutes. It took her the next three weeks to painstakingly draw the pictures. We still have the book. It's a masterpiece for a seven-year-old, but more a testimony to her artistic ability than to anything she learned about good writing. As I turn the pages of that book these many years later, I still wonder what else she might have learned about reading and writing in all the time she devoted to this non-academic dimension of this task.

Not only do kids love those boxes of crayons and their markers in so many colors, teachers like them, too. They keep kids quiet and busy.

And if you don't look too closely, those pretty pictures relate to the lesson objective. Or do they?

WHAT ABOUT THE LEVEL OF CLASSROOM TALK?

Many teachers will tell you that the kids in their room already talk too much, so getting them to talk more hardly seems a priority. However, it's not really about the quantity of talk, but the quality. Teachers who care what kids think do more than just give them time to express their thinking. They actively teach students to converse. They help students access the kind of academic vocabulary they need to talk about their reading like readers and their writing like writers. Then they expect students to use that language in well-constructed sentences appropriate to a classroom discussion.

When I enter some classrooms and gather a group of students to talk about a text, it feels like I am sitting down alongside a group of my peers. They slide into their seats like they do this on a regular basis (which they probably do), open their books—which often have more sticky notes poking out of pages than I have in my own book—and wait expectantly for someone (not necessarily the teacher) to say something to begin the dialogue.

"I never expected this character to persevere under such difficult circumstances," Monique, a fifth grader, offered.

"She did show amazing determination," Jake affirmed. "But didn't you think the author foreshadowed this outcome with evidence earlier in the book?" He flipped to one of his pages marked with a sticky note. "Here, listen to this…"

Martin, Destinee, and Charles later weighed in on the issue. One of them eventually did ask my opinion, though this didn't figure strongly in their own view of this chapter. These fifth graders had obviously developed a facility with academic language and the skills to talk about their reading in a scholarly manner. They knew specific terms to describe character traits: *persevere, determination.* They were familiar with literary terms: *foreshadow, outcome, evidence.* They easily referenced their text with strategically placed sticky notes. They also knew how to listen to each other and how to disagree respectfully. No one needed my approval to feel confident in their interpretation of the text, nor did they require my permission before sharing their thinking. I love to work in classrooms such as this one, where the art of conversation has been deliberately taught, where response is focused on the substance and articulation of the thought.

In other classrooms, academic talk means responding to teachers' questions, mostly of the recall variety. The goal is to be the first kid to get called on because there's only one right answer and, as soon as the teacher gets the correct response, she's on to the next question.

These fifth graders had obviously developed a facility with academic language and the skills to talk about their reading in a scholarly manner.

I love to work in classrooms such as this one, where the art of conversation has been deliberately taught, where response is focused on the substance and articulation of the thought.

Thinking is more aligned with competition than collaboration. In too many cases, a single word or simple phrase gets the job done. Students are not even required to reply in complete sentences. They mumble. Their language is imprecise and limited: The character is *nice*, or *bad*, or *happy*. In classrooms where conversation is not celebrated, fewer children are willing to risk responding at all. I ask a question. A tentative hand goes up. After the responder answers, he awaits my approving nod and you can almost hear an audible sigh of relief when the answer is accepted.

ARE THE MATERIALS ORGANIZED FOR EASY ACCESS?

In the earlier part of this chapter, I talked about the accessibility of students' books as an essential feature of the classroom environment. What about the teacher's resources? Are they accessible? Can she find them when she needs them? Are they nicely laid out so she can easily put her hand on just what she needs at a given moment? Or are books and papers scattered from one end of the classroom to another, hidden among other books and papers that look *almost* like the one she is looking for...but no, that's not the one.

Good teachers somehow handle all of this, even with multiple groups reading multiple texts. They've also checked their technology before the lesson begins to be sure the bulb in the overhead projector is functioning, that the DVD player is in working order, and that their extension cord is long enough. How many times have I been in a classroom when teaching comes to a screeching halt, sometimes for many minutes, while the teacher hunts down someone who can figure out why, for example, the television monitor is producing sound but no picture.

IS THE EMOTIONAL CLIMATE OF THE CLASSROOM POSITIVE AND LOW RISK?

Some teachers are naturally warm and fuzzy while others are more matter-of-fact. While we can't change a teacher's personality, all teachers need to recognize that their interactions with students make their classroom a positive (or negative) place for children to be. Does the teacher resolve problems with students through reasoning and joint problem solving, or by screaming and threatening them into submission? Do students perceive that everyone in the class is treated equally and fairly, or do some members of the class appear to get special treatment?

When I enter some classrooms, I have to look hard before I even find the teacher. He is folded into a pint-sized chair conversing quietly with a child. They are smiling at each other, as together they turn the pages of the book.

While we can't change a teacher's personality, all teachers need to recognize that their interactions with students make their classroom a positive (or negative) place for children to be.

There are other situations where I hear the teacher's booming voice long before I arrive at the classroom door. She is reprimanding one child or another for some rule infraction. I remember having a teacher like that myself a long time ago. Although I learned a lot from this woman, my most enduring memory is of the anxiety I felt over things that matter a lot to a ten-year-old: *Would Ms. L take my new pen away if my handwriting wasn't neat enough, as she had taken my friend's new pen? What if I got the lowest grade on the social studies test? Everyone would know because my paper would be the last one in the pile to be returned. This was a high-risk classroom and I had a stomach ache to prove it!*

Good teachers are aware of the emotional impact of their management strategies and try to correct them when necessary. A new teacher with whom I worked met with me before I visited her classroom one day and talked at length about how disrespectful her students were to her—and what was wrong with these kids, anyway?

"What is wrong was evident right away," I told the teacher after I had visited her classroom. "When you responded to your students' questions, there was an 'edginess' to your voice. It didn't sound like you really respected *them*." In so many ways, students take on the personal attributes of the teachers who teach them.

WHAT ABOUT TRANSITIONS?

Some teachers handle instruction masterfully, but when the lesson is over and students move to the next item on the daily agenda, there is too much noise and confusion. It's like rush hour without a traffic flow pattern. The two little boys who had absolutely nothing to say during the shared-reading lesson are now hollering insults at each other across the classroom. There have been times when I have literally jumped out of the way as students hurtled down the stairs on their way to lunch. Transitions can get ugly.

Good teachers know they need to take these transitional moments in hand and come up with a system for monitoring students' behavior—or better yet, getting students to monitor their own behavior.

Good teachers know they need to take these transitional moments in hand and come up with a system for monitoring students' behavior—or better yet, getting students to monitor their own behavior. Anything the literacy coach can do to suggest management strategies for transitions or any other area of classroom management will, of course, be helpful. However, classroom management should not really be the domain of the literacy coach. The literacy coach should be working on *literacy*. Once basic issues of classroom management have been addressed (possibly with the assistance of a building administrator or other support staff), the coach's time in a classroom will be much more productive in helping the teacher refine instructional literacy practices. You will find a checklist for classroom management among the protocols in **Chapter Seven**.

STUDY QUESTIONS FOR CHAPTER ONE

1. Which features of the classroom environment described here do you consider most essential? Which do you consider "nice," but negotiable? Are there any that you think are completely unnecessary? Explain.

2. How should features of the classroom environment change as you move from the primary grades to the intermediate grades? Are there particular features that should be present in a middle-school literacy classroom?

3. How could you make "the classroom environment" a school-wide initiative in your building?

4. Which teacher(s) in your building have created classroom environments that could be shared with other teachers? How could you set up opportunities for such sharing without causing resentment toward these teachers?

5. Which aspects of classroom management do you think get in the way of literacy teaching and learning most significantly? Explain.

6. Do you think the literacy coach should work in (or be asked to work in) classrooms where a lack of classroom management is pre-empting literacy instruction? Under what circumstances might it be useful for a coach to work with a teacher with poor classroom-management skills?

2

Setting the Stage for Literacy Learning

Setting the stage for learning means motivating learners, activating and building background knowledge, and identifying objectives. Teachers often give too little attention to this instructional phase because to them it doesn't really feel like "teaching." After all, at this point they are delivering no new content to students.

But this step is critical to later learning. In fact, research says that setting the stage for learning is the single most important part of the lesson for struggling readers, especially when the reading is nonfiction like social studies or science texts.

So exactly what should we look for as we watch a teacher set the stage in a literacy lesson? First, picture the classroom. Let's imagine it's a third-grade classroom. The teacher is sitting in a not-quite-adult-sized chair in the front of the room, a flip chart next to her on an easel, surrounded by children seated on a rug. Good teachers know that no third graders (or students of any grade) are going to sit quietly on that rug indefinitely. The entire lesson can't take longer than twenty to thirty minutes. That means each component within this first phase must move along quickly for a total of about five to seven minutes. Begin by noticing what teachers do to get students to care.

Getting Students to Care

TIME FRAME: ONE TO TWO MINUTES

Unless kids care about learning, there is little point in moving forward with instruction. In some classrooms, this is not an issue. But getting kids motivated can be one of the greatest challenges a teacher faces. Children's heads may be lying on their desks. They might actually be asleep, or maybe they're simply too disinterested or too tuned out from fear of failure to rouse themselves from their lethargy. Others are so busy poking classmates and arguing that they don't even hear the teacher's repeated pleas to quiet down.

Several specific things coaches should look for as teachers initiate their lesson are described below, followed by what is evident when *getting students to care* goes off track. Some self-reflection questions for teachers for this portion of the lesson follow.

WHAT GOOD TEACHERS DO TO GET STUDENTS TO CARE

Good teachers actively motivate their students to care. They recognize that part of their job is cheerleading! Skip the pom-poms and pyramids, but do whatever it takes to convey to students that they will absolutely, no question about it, be successful with this new thing they're learning today if they just give it a chance. They may not be perfect, but they'll be way better at it than they are right now—and you PROMISE that you will be there to help and to make sure they succeed. Large measures of enthusiasm make this message convincing.

Good teachers explain *why* this new learning is important and *how* it will make life easier and better—right now: "You will definitely get a higher grade on Friday's social studies test if you pay attention to what we're discussing this morning about main ideas and details."

Good teachers require their students to focus and don't move on with their lesson until they have everyone's attention. Simple things like eye contact, tracking the speaker, good posture, and appropriate body language demonstrate a readiness for learning. No apathy allowed here!

When possible, good teachers lure learners with some concrete object related to the content of their lesson. "Did you ever see a rock like this?" a colleague of mine asked her seventh graders as she introduced a unit on geology. She passed the rock around so students could examine it for themselves. Even big kids thrive on real-life objects they can touch, as well as maps and other visuals.

WHAT YOU MIGHT SEE WHEN GETTING STUDENTS TO CARE GOES OFF TRACK

The most obvious "derailment" of this portion of the lesson is when teachers fail to acknowledge it and move ahead with their instruction as if it didn't matter. Chatter, heads on desks, noisily munching on chips or celery sticks, distracting requests ("Can I go to the lav?")—the instructional show still goes on with no clear standards for student behavior.

Some teachers attempt to gain control by threatening or by setting a negative tone: "This is hard, and if you don't listen, you're not going to get it." The only word students hear is *hard*; they shut down. Or, teachers project the benefits of the lesson somewhere in the distant future: "You're really going to need to understand outlining when you

> Good teachers require their students to focus and don't move on with their lesson until they have everyone's attention.

go to college." These are kids for whom "after lunch" seems a long way off. Improving their life ten years from now is not something they spend time worrying about.

And then there are the teachers who stand before their class and initiate their lesson in a flat, monotone voice that would put anyone to sleep. How can we expect children to be excited about learning when the teacher is bored?

ASK THE TEACHER:

- How do you get your students to tune in to instruction when you begin your lesson?
- What do you do about the kid who isn't paying attention or the child who is disruptive?
- How do you get students to believe they will be successful with new learning?
- What routines have you established to minimize time lost to classroom management?

Activating and Building Background Knowledge

TIME FRAME: THREE TO FIVE MINUTES

The students are still on the rug—or focused on the teacher from their desks.

WHAT GOOD TEACHERS DO TO ACTIVATE OR TO BUILD BACKGROUND KNOWLEDGE

When a good teacher is introducing something for the first time, such as a reading strategy, he finds a way to link the new learning to something that students already know. "What comprehension strategies have we talked about already?" the teacher might ask. Students respond, and the teacher continues: "Today, we're going to learn another strategy called *wondering* that will also help us with our reading." Good teachers know that learning proceeds more efficiently if they can get students to use their schema—the information that is safely tucked away in their mental filing cabinet—to connect what is known to what is new.

When good teachers are teaching a follow-up lesson, they build off of the previous day's content. "What did we learn about *wondering* yesterday? Who can tell me one thing that you remember about *wondering*?" Phrasing the question in this way is very smart of the teacher because telling *one thing* is less risky than if she had asked, "What is the *most important* thing we learned yesterday?"

Good teachers realize that listening to a few connections is sufficient to set the stage for learning. And you need to stick to the topic. They remember that the point of accessing this prior knowledge is to get to the text or the skill. They note when there's insufficient prior knowledge, and either 1) abort the mission, 2) set a slightly different course, temporarily modifying their objective, or 3) spend a bit more time actually *building* the necessary knowledge base. This can be tricky because teachers often cannot abandon a particular text or topic simply because students don't have the prerequisite knowledge.

I once went into a fourth grade with the picture book *The Other Side* (Putnam, 2001) by Jacqueline Woodson that focuses on segregation in the South prior to the Civil Rights era. As I attempted to tease out how much students knew about this era, it became clear that they were confusing "Civil Rights" with the "Civil War." Then somehow George Washington's name came up and, after that, someone asked if this was when people got dressed up and threw "all that tea" into a harbor. I could tell we had a bit of work to do before getting to our story.

We put the book down and created a little timeline with different students representing George Washington, Abraham Lincoln, and Martin Luther King, Jr. "Look, this guy here was dead before this one was even born," I told them. "George Washington" got to go back to his seat. "And then there was Abe…and after a while, Martin." We were now a day behind in our work, but at least everyone had acquired a general sense of the right century. We could address the lesson's objective, noticing details that supported a conclusion, when we read the book the next day.

Good teachers also know that they need to activate prior knowledge about more than just the topic. What do students know about the author? What do they know about the genre or text structure?

Good teachers also know that they need to activate prior knowledge about more than just the topic. What do students know about the author? What do they know about the genre or text structure? "This story was written by Kevin Henkes," I told a class of kindergarteners, holding up the book *Owen*. "Did we read any other books by this author?

"*Chrysanthemum!*" announced one of several toothless five-year-olds, doing the best she could with that hard-to-pronounce word.

"So what might we find in this book," I continued, "since it was written by Kevin Henkes?"

"Sad feelings and then happy feelings," a little boy with big brown eyes replied, making an appropriately sad face. Even young students can comprehend the relevance of an author (or genre) to get their minds ready to read.

Good teachers remember to front-load a few vocabulary words with some content significance to support the later reading and to stretch their students' oral and written vocabularies. They stay away from basic high-frequency words (*the*, *was*, *when*) and also technical language that children will have little opportunity to use beyond the confines of a given text (*isthmus*, *archetype*). They select only a couple of words—terms students will be able to use to understand the text better—and incorporate into their speaking and writing vocabularies—*dreadful*, *talent*, *galloping*.

WHAT YOU MIGHT SEE WHEN ACTIVATING AND BUILDING PRIOR KNOWLEDGE GOES OFF TRACK

There's been so much attention to the value of prior knowledge in literacy development that sometimes teachers go overboard in celebrating kids' connections. This can take forever, gobbles up valuable time that could be spent reading, and often actually diverts attention from the topic at hand. Or, they may deliver a lengthy monologue with no opportunity for interaction or student input that can quickly lead to fidgety kids who change their mental channels from "reading lesson" to "soccer after school."

You may also see teachers activating or building background knowledge that is not really essential to the reading or getting caught up in text details that are only marginally significant. I recently taught a first-grade demonstration lesson about the first lunar landing. Because it was early in the year, the six-year-olds really had to stretch to grasp even the basics of this historic event. During the debriefing that followed, one of the teachers who had observed the lesson was clearly disenchanted. "What's wrong?" I asked her.

"You didn't activate enough background knowledge," she replied. "You didn't tell them where Houston was."

Houston? I considered it a very good day when these six-year-olds could tell me at the end of the lesson that three men flew in a rocket ship all the way to the moon, planted an American flag, collected some rocks, and returned safely to earth. A discussion of the Houston Space Center could be saved for another day.

Some teachers also need to rethink their introduction of vocabulary. Presenting a laundry list of new words can consume endless minutes—and students can't absorb more than a couple of words at one time, anyway.

Ignoring signs that students are lost is one of the worst mistakes teachers can make during this phase of the lesson. This will happen at other points during a lesson, too, but teachers would do well to recognize the early signs. Some teachers see that students are lost (or maybe they miss these obvious cues), and keep chugging along. This is how the achievement gap widens! When a student misses an important first step, there is no foundation on which to build later learning.

When a student misses an important first step, there is no foundation on which to build later learning.

- What kinds of background knowledge do you think are important to activate?
- What kind of background knowledge seems to help your students the most?
- How much time do you spend reviewing your previous lesson?
- When you see that your students don't have enough prior knowledge on a topic, what do you do then?
- What do you do when too many students want to share their personal connections (prior knowledge)?
- When you teach vocabulary, how do you choose your words? How many words do you introduce at one time?

Identifying Objectives

TIME FRAME: ONE MINUTE OR LESS

This is quick!

WHAT GOOD TEACHERS DO TO IDENTIFY OBJECTIVES

Good teachers have one—and only one—clearly defined (and important) lesson objective. Other points can be made during the reading as they come up and seem appropriate, but focusing on a single, clear objective is best. A valuable objective should relate to a grade-level standard, and it should be applied to the curriculum in an authentic way. It should also be measurable. Here's an example: One of our state literacy standards requires that "Students will make a personal connection to a text explaining how an experience of theirs was like or different from an experience of a story character." That is something that can easily be applied to shared, guided, and independent reading—not just to a test-prep passage—and is something all students should be able to do. Other examples of worthy objectives might be to write an attention-getting story lead, to segment words into their onset and rime (c + at = cat), or to infer an author's message.

Good teachers at all levels make sure that students know what the objective is. They state the objective in language that their students can readily understand and they make sure the objective is measurable. "Find two details that show that Tomás was brave" is more measurable and meaningful than "Find details to support a conclusion." Now students know what they are proving, and they know how many details are needed. If possible, include a number in a specific objective!

Good teachers post their objectives for students to reference visually. I encourage teachers to post the objective in the same place in the classroom each time and to use an identifying icon, like a bulls-eye, to make it easy to find it. Some teachers with more artistic ability than I possess invent little cartoon characters and give them names. In one third grade I visited, the teacher kept telling her students to check with Geraldine before handing in their assignment. It took me several minutes to figure out that Geraldine was the young lady with spiky purple hair affixed to the wall advertising the day's writing objective.

Good teachers remind students that they *will* be held accountable at the end of the lesson. *Well, of course they know they're accountable,* you're probably thinking. Still, this sometimes comes as a surprise to students.

"Today I'm going to show you how to revise your writing by adding color words. What do you think I'm going to ask *you* to do after I finish showing you how to do this in a piece of *my* writing?" I asked a group of first graders. A few hands shot up to answer my question, but not as many as I anticipated.

WHAT YOU MIGHT SEE WHEN IDENTIFYING OBJECTIVES GOES OFF TRACK

You might not see any objective at all. You might notice that the objective is really an activity: *narrative writing* or *guided reading*.

Or, you might see that the objective relates only to the content of a text and not to improving students' skills and strategies as readers and writers: "Today's objective: Read **Chapter 3** and answer the questions." This teacher is teaching the *reading*, and not the *reader*.

You might even wonder why a teacher would choose this particular objective at all. For example, a good objective for a fluency lesson is definitely not (as I once noted in a teacher's lesson plan) asking students to read an entire paragraph without taking a breath. If students pass out before reaching the end of their passage, it may be a bit difficult to measure their growth!

Other teachers may aim too broadly and "teach fuzzy." For example, a teacher I once observed proudly displayed a chart she had developed as a part of planning her demonstration lesson. "Look at all the objectives we met today," she announced, pointing to about a dozen circled items on the state literacy framework list. The problem is that she didn't really teach for the mastery of any objective; she touched upon several things, but didn't address anything thoroughly.

And the worst potential pitfall of all: The lesson the teacher ultimately presents may not match the objective. But you won't know that until the next phase of instruction.

Good teachers remind students that they *will* be held accountable at the end of the lesson

ASK THE TEACHER:

- How do you determine your objective for a lesson?
- How do you communicate your objective to your students?
- How do you determine if your objective is a worthy one?
- Creating measurable objectives can be challenging. What do you consider when trying to make your objective measurable?

In about five to seven minutes, the teacher should have set the stage for learning by motivating students, encouraging them to think about what they already know, and helping them to understand the learning objective. It didn't take up the entire lesson time, and the students are now ready for some new content. See the check sheet in Chapter Seven for Setting the Stage for Literacy to reflect on the specifics of this phase of literacy instruction in your own classroom or the classroom of a teacher you are coaching.

STUDY QUESTIONS FOR CHAPTER TWO

1. Think of a few statements teachers can use to express their unwavering belief that students will succeed. (Examples: "I can tell by the way you're paying such close attention today that this is going to be easy for you; You are so smart. Some [third] graders might have trouble with this, but you have already shown me. . .")

2. Identify some hands-on items that could support particular lessons.

3. What else can we do as teachers to more effectively hold students' attention through positive reinforcement?

4. Select a picture book, story from your core program, or some other text. Choose a few vocabulary words to introduce from this text over an entire week. Consider the language needs of your particular students when making your selection. Try not to choose words that are too technical.

5. Where do you think teachers are most likely to go off track as they set the stage for literacy learning? Why do you think this is happening? What do teachers need to know about literacy instruction in order to improve their capacity to set the stage for learning?

6. Do you think a timer would be helpful in keeping teachers on track during this and other parts of a literacy lesson? Discuss the pros and cons.

3

Building Knowledge

Building knowledge is the second phase of explicit instruction and is what some would consider the "meat and potatoes course" on the literacy menu. The important tasks of explaining, modeling, and bridging should take about fifteen to twenty minutes, and they need to be executed carefully if teachers hope to move students toward mastery and independence. Teachers readily acknowledge the significance of this phase of explicit instruction, and most often genuinely believe they implement the tasks well. This, however, is not always the case; explaining and modeling are trickier than they appear on the surface.

Bridging is the final, trickiest, and possibly most-neglected part of this phase of the gradual release model. A very structured kind of supported practice, bridging provides a critical link between the teaching and the learning. The explicit monitoring that is part of the bridging component allows teachers to take a serious look at how comfortable students are with the new learning. The knowledge that teachers gain about student performance level at this point during the instruction will be important as they plan for guided and independent practice in the final instructional phase, described in **Chapter Four**.

The specific components of instruction and teacher reflection questions in this chapter will show you how to help teachers—even veteran teachers—fine-tune their capacity to help children build new knowledge efficiently.

Explaining

TIME FRAME: TWO TO THREE MINUTES

A good explanation is a beautiful thing. We expect teachers to explain things clearly in language appropriate to their particular grade level. But that is not enough. Good explanations go beyond telling students *what* to do. They also include the *how*. *How* do you locate the information you need to respond to a particular question—the main idea, details to support a conclusion, the most important part of a story? A good explanation helps students to think about their thinking: to be metacognitive.

WHAT GOOD TEACHERS DO TO EXPLAIN

When I ask coaches to tell me how they might help teachers explain a particular strategy to their students, such as, how to identify the most important part of a story, there is a lot of dead air. The fact is that explaining something often *seems* easy until we need to convert the explanation to language that a young child will understand.

Good teachers realize that providing a good explanation means offering up a few "hot tips" or hints for succeeding at the task. They need to translate the thinking they do so automatically as adults to a more intentional process that they can describe clearly to their students. Good explanations help students strategize and gain control over the task. To return to our previous example, once students know what counts as "most important" in a story, finding that evidence and identifying related details becomes relatively easy. Furthermore, without thoughtful explanations, it is difficult for students to apply today's learning to similar tasks in the future.

The value and content of a good explanation is not something that most teachers—or even most coaches—think about on a regular basis. What does a good explanation sound like?

A good explanation is brief. It recognizes that short-term memory is easily overloaded and mentions just a few hints to focus students' thinking: "The most important part of a story might be where the author is describing the problem, where a character changes, or where the problem gets solved. When you're looking for story elements, remember that the author usually describes the characters, setting, and problem near the *beginning* of the story." There's always tomorrow to add a few more nuggets of wisdom.

Likewise, good teachers recognize that, although they are primarily responsible for this part of the lesson and are doing most of the talking themselves, students need to be brought into the process, if only in small ways.

First, children easily lose their focus when they are not actively engaged, and just listening doesn't constitute active engagement for many students. Also, even small amounts of input from children will provide a teacher with valuable insights into what they know about a skill or strategy. When I was modeling "good explaining" in a fifth-grade class recently, I began by asking instead of telling: "What do *you* think could be the most important part of a story?"

With a little guidance, the students produced their own "explanation" of how to strategize about finding the most important part of a story.

Good teachers realize that providing a good explanation means offering up a few "hot tips" or hints for succeeding at the task.

With a little guidance, the students produced their own "explanation" of how to strategize about finding the most important part of a story.

WHAT YOU MIGHT SEE WHEN EXPLAINING GOES OFF TRACK

Commonly, you'll see directions, not explanations: "Here's how you complete this worksheet. Draw a line from the word in column A to the picture that matches it in column B." Researcher Dolores Durkin found many years ago that teachers did more "mentioning" than actual "teaching" when it came to comprehension. She might well find the same thing today.

Even very good teachers sometimes have a hard time with this. Two of my favorite literacy coaches were eager to show me their video of a lesson they had modeled in a fourth-grade classroom. The objective of the lesson was for students to identify the main idea in a piece of informational text.

"Watch how I underline just the sentence that the article is *mainly about*," one of the coaches told the class." The camera then zoomed in as she did exactly what she had described—underlined the main idea statement.

When the video was over, the coaches were eager for my feedback. "What did you think?" they wanted to know. It's always hard to be honest when you know how badly a teacher or coach wants to hear your words of praise, and the performance wasn't quite as praiseworthy as intended. I started by saying something positive about another part of the lesson that truly was excellent, but then I had to find a gentle way of delivering the not-so-good news.

"You told them *what* to do and *where* you found the main idea statement, but did you let them know *how* you found the main idea so they could do it themselves afterward?"

"Oh," they sighed. "But what would a good explanation of finding the main idea look like?"

"There are lots of hints you could give students," I offered. "Different strategies will work with different texts." I looked at the passage they had used. It was from a social studies chapter about westward expansion and was an easy one to use to explain main idea because it had so many of the traditional expository text features.

"I would explain to students that if *I* were looking for a main idea in a paragraph, I know I might not find it stated directly in the text. I would look for clues that could help me figure out the main idea. In this text, I am lucky because there are subtitles for each paragraph: *Women's Work in the Old West, Men's Work in the Old West, Children's Work in the Old West.* That will let me know what the author is going to describe about life in the Old West. I could probably create a main idea statement for each paragraph by first turning the subtitle into a question: *What kind of work do women do on the homestead?* The answer to that question is the main idea!"

> Different strategies will work with different texts.

Not all informational text will be set up so conveniently with chapter titles and subtitles, so tomorrow I might provide a few additional hints (*Read the first paragraph. Read the first sentence of each succeeding paragraph. Read the last paragraph.*) None of these tricks of the trade will work every time. But if students have enough strategies in their bag of tricks, they will know their options when they are asked to find a main idea.

It's tough not only to identify what goes into a good explanation, but also to say it in language that children can understand. As capable adult readers and writers, we do these things almost automatically—summarize text, determine the lesson a story teaches, write an attention-grabbing lead to a letter. When we try to break that process down and put it into words that a six – or sixteen-year-old can understand, we realize how challenging it is to offer high-quality explanations that are both simple and precise.

Occasionally the explanation seems to go on and on and on, almost interminably: "First you do this. Then comes this step. After that…" The teacher crams so much into it that you know it will take days to navigate all of the steps—with most children left behind at step number one. I once watched a teacher explain the format of an essay to her fifth graders for the first time:

"First write your introductory paragraph. That should include your topic with your three main ideas stated. Next, begin your first main body paragraph with a topic sentence followed by three details, all supported with elaboration, and don't forget a concluding sentence. Remember that your main body paragraphs need at least five sentences each." She rattled on about the remaining three paragraphs as well. But my mind was still trying to process the information about the essay introduction. Indeed, teachers who explain well know that a good explanation is a short explanation.

ASK THE TEACHER:
- How did you explain _____?
- What did you suggest to students for succeeding at this skill or strategy?
- How long did it take you to explain this?
- How did you keep students engaged in this part of the lesson?
- How did you decide when it was time to move on to modeling?

Modeling

TIME FRAME: FOUR TO FIVE MINUTES

A teacher who models well is adequately prepared. If the teacher is using a text to model, you will be able to tell that he read the book beforehand to get ready for this lesson. He has a plan in mind. This will be apparent from the way he has carefully segmented the text, where he stops to think aloud, and the quality of the thinking he models. Ideally, there will be an actual written lesson plan as well that you can look at to get a sense of the overall lesson organization.

WHAT GOOD TEACHERS DO TO MODEL

The text will be a good match for the strategy the teacher has just explained with multiple opportunities to demonstrate it. For example, fables are a useful genre when you're trying to figure out an author's message or the lesson a story teaches. Realistic fiction is perfect for making personal connections. Adventure stories are great for wondering what will happen next and making predictions. The teacher will stop to think aloud a sufficient number of times to show the strategy in action—but not so often that the continuity of the story is destroyed.

Good teachers make their use of the strategy appear spontaneous, as if it is happening in "real time" so that students will see how they can apply this in the same way as they do their own reading: "Right here on this page I'm wondering why Little Red Riding Hood is talking to the wolf. She should know better than to speak to strangers. On this page I'm noticing that Granny looks a lot like the wolf. I'm wondering why Little Red Riding Hood doesn't notice this, too."

While much modeling is oral, there may also be a written component. This is especially true for writing lessons. "Let me show you how I add suspense to my story," the teacher may say. "Watch how I revise my writing to include a size word," a first-grade teacher tells her class, and then demonstrates on the white board exactly what she means: "The *gigantic* black bear walked slowly through the forest." The modeling that the teacher does is clear and confirms her solid grasp of the skill, strategy, or concept she is communicating to her students.

> Most importantly, good teachers make sure that the modeling is linked to the explanation that preceded it so students can readily see how the strategy works.

Most importantly, good teachers make sure that the modeling is linked to the explanation that preceded it so students can readily see how the strategy works: "Remember that we just talked about words that good questions often begin with—*who, what, when, where, why, how*. Notice how the questions I'm asking about this story begin with some of those words." Students need to see the thinking behind the modeling in order to be able to transfer "teacher talk" to their own learning.

WHAT YOU MIGHT SEE WHEN MODELING GOES OFF TRACK

You may not see any modeling at all and notice that a teacher tries to move directly from explaining to independent reading or writing. But this is becoming less and less likely. Modeling has gained great favor in recent years and is now a staple of literacy instruction in many classrooms. The problem is that teachers' modeling is sometimes sloppy and doesn't serve any real purpose.

Some teachers pluck a book off a shelf two minutes before the lesson begins as if all texts were created equal for modeling different skills and strategies. I once watched a kindergarten teacher do a lovely lesson on the "B" sound as an initial consonant. She then grabbed the nearest picture book and started reading aloud, confident, I'm sure, that there would be plenty of Bs to highlight. Well, there weren't. In fact, there were almost no Bs at all. The teacher was embarrassed because it was obvious to us both that she hadn't planned very well.

Perhaps the most common problem I witness is modeling that goes on and on without any guidance to help students process what they are observing. These teachers seem to think that the thinking aloud itself is instructive—even fascinating—to their students. They only model the *application* of the strategy: "Here's where I'm making a connection"; "Here's where I'm wondering about something I'm reading." There's no effort to explain *how* they got that connection or *why* that was a good place to stop and wonder.

Occasionally teachers will stop to model so frequently that it ruins the continuity of the story.

More modeling is not necessarily *better* modeling. I once watched a teacher model her thinking about comprehension strategies as she read aloud *The Relatives Came* (Cynthia Rylant) to her second graders. She modeled every one of her personal connections, everything she pictured on each page, all of the questions that popped into her mind, and multiple examples of author's craft. By the time she got to the middle of the book, the students had lost all sense of the story itself.

Good modeling is selective. It notes just a few places within a text where the story comes to life through the application of the *best* connections, mental pictures, predictions, etc. Good modeling does not get in the way of the enjoyment of the adventure or the humor or the message that the story conveys.

A more subtle modeling error is a teacher's reliance on the past tense: "When I read this book last night I was thinking about how my life was a lot like this character's life…" Modeling isn't about what you did last night or some time in the past; it's about what you are thinking right now at this exact minute. We want students to see how we actively engage with text in the present, while we are reading, because that's what we want them to do, too.

You may find that sometimes a teacher is oblivious to distracted or disengaged students. The teacher reads page after page as the kids wiggle and squirm, looking out the window or playing with the Velcro on their sneakers. I've heard administrators make this situation worse

More modeling is not necessarily *better* modeling.

Good modeling does not get in the way of the enjoyment of the adventure or the humor or the message that the story conveys.

by telling teachers they should model for several days (even weeks) before turning the task over to students. I disagree. Modeling should be brief and focused, just a few minutes at a time. The teacher should always be watching for signs that her students are "getting it." Within any lesson, the teacher should move beyond his solo performance to student participation.

Most disturbing of all is the teacher who misrepresents or does not really understand the concept she is trying to demonstrate. I remember listening to a teacher's explanation once of a Venn diagram, thinking it was a little off track—or maybe I just wasn't listening closely enough. Then she modeled. *Oh, no,* I silently groaned. *She's got this all wrong.* That time, I hoped that students' minds *were* wandering so they would not need to unlearn this misinformation.

ASK THE TEACHER:
- How did you choose the text you used for modeling?
- How did you decide where to stop and think aloud?
- About how many times did you stop to think aloud?
- How could you tell whether or not your modeling was effective?
- What did students do as you continued to model?

Bridging

TIME FRAME: SEVEN TO TEN MINUTES

A bridge connects two things that would otherwise remain separated. In this case, we are attempting to bridge teaching and learning, connecting what the teacher has been doing (mostly by himself) to what students will now do (mostly by themselves). In this middle ground, teachers and students jointly engage in the task.

WHAT GOOD TEACHERS DO TO BRIDGE

Good teachers accomplish bridging by paying close attention to who is succeeding at the task and ready to engage in similar work independently, who is on the cusp of understanding and in need of just a little additional guidance in order to reach mastery, and who is still in need of extensive teacher support or re-teaching. In this way, bridging provides the information the teacher needs to plan and differentiate the instruction that follows.

Bridging is tricky because it is not an entirely discrete instructional component. A teacher begins to explain something, and then the explanation is complete and she moves on to modeling. But modeling doesn't come to an abrupt halt so bridging can begin. Good teachers watch for signs as they model that their students are catching on. They read the smile of recognition on their faces and the gleam in their eyes. They watch for hands waving, tentatively at first, and then more confidently, to share their own thinking. They take a baby step and ask for a student's input on a very small point initially, gradually incorporating the thinking of more and more students in more substantial ways.

Sometimes it's hard for a coach or other classroom visitor to identify the precise moment when modeling ends and bridging begins. And that's okay. The important thing is that good teachers *do* make an effort to bridge and that it is this component of instruction that accounts for the most minutes in any explicit lesson.

Another reason it is sometimes difficult to distinguish this bridging component is that, if a text is used, it is generally the same one that was used for modeling. Maybe the teacher read the first half of a picture book and modeled the strategy with her own thinking aloud. As she moves on to the second half of the book, she begins to incorporate students' thinking.

Good teachers know that bridging requires careful prompting of students' thinking in a step-by-step manner: "What's the first thing we do when we want to understand a character?"

"That's right. We can see what the character *says*. Who can find an example of this in our story?"

"What else can we check to learn about a character?"

"Good. We can notice the person's actions. Can someone find a place in our story where the character is *doing* something that shows what is important to her?"

No one is allowed to stray too far from success as good teachers bridge to greater student independence. Similarly, good teachers know that bridging means *many* repetitions: "Tell me what you're thinking, Josh. Now you tell me your thinking, Tricia." The teacher calls on several students to provide a response to the same basic question. It is this repeated practice that makes the learning permanent.

You will also note that good teachers hold children to high standards even in their first attempts at meeting a new objective. "I love the way Quinn gave his answer in a complete sentence and used our new vocabulary word meaningfully."

Now everyone knows what you're looking for right from the start. It's much harder, days or weeks later, to have to finally confess to students, "You know those answers you've been giving for the past couple of weeks—well, they were never actually very good. But I didn't want to hurt your feelings."

Measuring student progress in meeting a lesson's objective is the best way to assess whether the teacher has bridged adequately. Refer to the target set during the first phase of instruction. What were students expected to do at the conclusion of the lesson? Can they do it?

Suppose the target was for kindergarten students to put three events from a story in order or to picture something described in a story using size and color words. Ask them to do this orally. The teacher won't be able to listen to every child's response, but a representative sample of answers from different children in the class will afford a general sense of who "gets it" and who doesn't.

This is important because the shared portion of the lesson is now over. In the final phase of instruction, the teacher will need to know just how much scaffolding is still needed by his students so he can differentiate the instruction that will get everyone to independence as efficiently as possible.

Finally, a good teacher uses the bridge to prepare students for the next phase of instruction. This means setting the agenda for guided and independent practice, described in greater detail in the following chapter. For now, think about how effortlessly some teachers get kids to move from one activity to the next and from one place in the classroom to another. *That's* what coaches are hoping to see as teachers wrap up the shared portion of the literacy block and move students toward *reinforcing knowledge*.

WHAT YOU MIGHT SEE WHEN BRIDGING GOES OFF TRACK

Some teachers neglect this important instructional component because they are not as aware of the role of bridging as they should be. In some cases, though, omitting this piece is actually intentional. I've had some heated discussions with teachers who staunchly maintain that this bridging thing isn't such a big deal. They've seen videos in which teachers of writing present a concept to students, model it in their own writing, and then set children free to try it on their own. I call this the "sink-or-swim" approach to teaching. Unfortunately, I can point to plenty of drowned students who prove this too true.

Bridging provides a "baby-step" support for students so they can eventually venture out on their own with less fear of failure. It's a shared teacher/class experience that guides, supports, and encourages, allowing them to experiment safely before trying something new by themselves.

Bridging also gives another learning opportunity to those students who may not "get it" yet. A teacher will not be fully aware of which children understand a new concept and which do not from modeling alone. Bridging time can help by giving *all* children needed time to practice the newly modeled strategy—many times.

The teacher won't be able to listen to every child's response, but a representative sample of answers from different children in the class will afford a general sense of who "gets it" and who doesn't.

Bridging provides a "baby-step" support for students so they can eventually venture out on their own with less fear of failure.

Sometimes teachers gloss over this portion of the lesson in a cursory fashion because the task seems so easy to them, whether it's summarizing a story, segmenting phonemes, or writing an introduction to a piece of narrative writing. Honestly, she may be a little bored by all of this practice and may worry that her students will be bored, too. Practice is not, however, boring to children who have never tried their hand at a particular strategy before, and it is certainly not easy for most of them.

When bridging has gone off track, students are not prepared to move on. They continue to be dependent on the teacher, which raises everyone's level of anxiety. The teacher is now frustrated because she has gotten to the end of the lesson and has finally figured out that she has a lot of "lost children." Many of the children can't respond to the question that measures the lesson's objective. They are anxious because they realize they will be unable to produce whatever the teacher has requested as a shared-lesson follow-up. The transition to the next activity does not feel orderly and comfortable, but rather, disorganized and too risky for some students. Before the teacher has even finished with the directions for what to do next, half the class is frantically flagging her down with those famous four words: *I don't get it.*

ASK THE TEACHER:

- How do you monitor who understands the process/skill/strategy and who doesn't understand it?
- How long does it generally take before students begin to share their thinking?
- Do you prompt students? How?
- What do you do if you can see that students are using a strategy inaccurately?
- How do you clarify the expectations for the final phase of the literacy block and help students transition to guided and independent reading and writing?

Study Questions for Chapter Three

1. List several objectives that a teacher might want to explain to students. For example, finding a new title for a text, determining what is important to a character or author, deciding why an author chose a specific genre, etc. Consider how you would explain how to meet each objective to students at your grade level.

2. What factors help to make modeling a success? How will you know when your modeling has actually been effective?

3. Share texts that you have used to model specific objectives. Why was each text a good match for the selected objective?

4. What will bridging look like in your classroom when you are teaching _____? (If a colleague came into your classroom during this portion of the lesson, what would she see?)

5. How can your monitor students' progress during bridging so you get an accurate sense of their progress?

6. How can the bridging portion of the lesson help you to differentiate your instruction later on?

4

Reinforcing Knowledge

Reinforcing knowledge involves guided practice, independent practice, and reflection. During this final phase, instruction is differentiated to meet the diverse needs of all students, and is where students learn to read by reading and to write by writing. Students engage in authentic follow-up activities to apply the objectives introduced in shared or guided reading. And finally, it is where teacher and students come back together at the end of the literacy block to think about their thinking one more time: What did we learn today that will make us better readers and writers?

Although reinforcing knowledge is just one of three parts of the gradual release model, it should actually consume two-thirds of the instructional time. At least one hour each day is needed for this phase of instruction; ninety minutes is even better.

Guided practice and independent practice happen at the same time and do not occur in any particular order. While some students are working in a small group with the teacher, others are engaged in independent reading and writing or follow-up applications. This configuration changes several times in a morning as groups of students move back and forth between instructional formats, both guided and independent.

Orchestrating these components is the greatest challenge teachers face in reinforcing knowledge. It's all about multi-tasking—or if you prefer a circus analogy, juggling several balls at one time.

"But what do the kids at their seats do when I'm working with a small group?" I wish I had a dime for every time a teacher has asked me that question during a workshop. This chapter will help you answer that question from the literacy coach's viewpoint and provide some reflection questions that can transform teachers into master multi-taskers.

Guided Practice

The goal of guided practice is to give students the opportunity to practice skills and strategies with *some* teacher in-put but with less direct support than they received during the bridging portion of the whole-class (shared) lesson. Ideally during guided practice, the teacher will reinforce the same objective introduced in the whole-class lesson, although realistically, this will not always work out. Instead, *any* objective from a previous lesson that meets students' needs would be appropriate. The exact focus should depend on areas of weakness that the teacher has observed in any dimension of literacy: oral language, phonemic awareness, phonics, fluency, vocabulary, or comprehension. The focus area might also relate to writing, though this will probably not occur as frequently and the guided practice may or may not take place in a group settting.

Remember that the emphasis here is *reinforcing* knowledge, not *building* knowledge. Note that the time frame for teachers is approximately one hour for this phase of instruction—or longer if the classroom schedule allows. Children, however, may be engaged in guided practice for only a fraction of this time, perhaps fifteen to twenty minutes. Note as well that guided practice, as it is defined here, is synonymous with small-group instruction that has a clear focus—one specific objective. It is not intended as a format for students simply to practice their reading. It is not "guided reading" the way it is typically packaged in many primary classrooms whereby the lesson begins with an extensive "picture-walk" laden with predictions, followed by whisper-reading, followed by a "strategy-booster."

WHAT GOOD TEACHERS DO TO PROVIDE GUIDED PRACTICE

Good teachers use-small group time to help differentiate learning for students who are performing at different levels. They provide students with texts they can read and work with at their own stage of reading development. The text poses some challenges but also the opportunity for achieving success when skills and strategies are applied accurately.

Good teachers draw on the power of small groups to promote the active engagement of *all* children, even those who lose focus during whole-group sessions; with only a few students gathered around the table, everyone can participate! Good teachers likewise take advantage of this small group setting to monitor students' progress thoroughly.

Good teachers focus on setting up groups for the practice of a previously learned skill or strategy, seldom to introduce a new one. Maybe the objective was introduced earlier this morning, or earlier this month, or much earlier in the year. For advanced readers, the teacher may wish to extend learning by refining a strategy or building on a previously introduced concept.

Good teachers have a clear, measurable objective and begin their small-group lesson by quickly motivating students and reviewing prior knowledge. They briefly revisit the strategy and devote the most time to student practice. Because there are fewer students to monitor, other instructional goals can sometimes be included as well, such as checking up on students' fluency or word-level knowledge. At the primary level, a few minutes of every small-group session should be devoted to sight-word instruction or review.

As a coach, you'll see good teachers capitalizing on small groups for high student engagement during guided practice. Rather than asking a series of questions that elicit a response from only one student before moving to the next question, good teachers encourage readers to construct their own meaning through a format that promotes discussion equally among everyone at the table.

Facilitating a really great discussion about a piece of literature or a content-area text is one of the hallmarks of teaching excellence and is a powerful part of the process that leads students toward independence.

Facilitating a really great discussion about a piece of literature or a content-area text is one of the hallmarks of teaching excellence and is a powerful part of the process that leads students toward independence. I love watching my colleague Laurie work with small groups in her third-grade classroom. First, she speaks to them like they are all friends she truly cares about as she gathers everyone together at the reading table. "How's it going, Louis?" she asks as this pint-sized lad slides into the seat next to her. "I was hoping I'd get to sit next to you today," she adds, pushing a pile of papers aside to make room for Louis's reading folder.

There's nothing too familiar about the interaction between teacher and students, but you just know they genuinely enjoy each other. The lack of formality sets a tone that helps kids feel comfortable. Sitting around this table doesn't feel risky at all. Louis (and his six classmates) will be willing to share their thinking about today's book because Laurie has worked hard to make everyone feel welcome and valued.

But positive small-group interaction goes beyond a sense of belonging. Laurie throws out the first comment to start the conversation. "Did anyone else get a really funny picture in your mind when you read the author's description of J. Pinkerton Silverfish?" The group was reading the first chapter of *Be a Perfect Person in Just Three Days* by Stephen Manes.

"I did," Vanessa offered right away. "I could especially picture the yellow mustard dribbling down his chin. Gross."

"I wondered why anyone would go to a doctor who looked like a clown," Jordan mused, referring to the red nose and mismatched shoes mentioned in the story.

"I think I have a connection," said Louis. "My doctor always wears a crazy tie and has a funny creature hooked to his stethoscope. Maybe he thinks this will make kids feel less scared when they're at the doctor's. It never worked with me when I was little, though."

Eventually everyone shared his or her thinking in the same way adult friends might share their thoughts in a book study around your dining room table. A rich conversation about this character developed without a single, direct question posed by the teacher. This is the kind of group activity and cross-dialogue that really does reinforce knowledge by guiding readers to more advanced levels of thinking. While all of this *looks* spontaneous, the truth is that facilitating a discussion this rich shows that the teacher has prepared carefully ahead of time. She has read the text herself. She has noted her own use of strategies. She knows how to say just enough to prompt students to activate their own thinking processes.

I heartily believe that guiding readers happens most efficiently and effectively in a small-group setting as opposed to one-on-one conferences between the teacher and individual students. That is because readers often "draft" their comprehension of text initially and then revise their thinking as they engage in conversations about what they have read with other readers. Good teachers make use of small-group interaction to lead readers to higher levels of thinking and recognize that there should be more student-talk than teacher-talk during small-group sessions.

Guiding writers, however, is different. While small groups of students can come together to reflect on a piece of writing, guidance for writers is typically provided most readily as teachers confer with students individually.

Picture this: A fifth-grade teacher has introduced a writing objective—for example, creating suspense by making each sentence in a paragraph successively shorter. She has explained the concept, modeled it, and invited students to help her create one or two additional examples together on the white board. Now it's time for students to try to write their own suspenseful paragraph using the same technique. The teacher criss-crosses the room, stopping to look over shoulders, confer briefly, and respond to questions.

"Listen to this!" she says after a quick glance at Ravi's paper. She proceeds to read the beginning of his paragraph aloud. It's a perfect example of building suspense by varying sentence lengths. As with small-group reading instruction, students have now been guided by a peer as well as by their teacher. But in this case, the guidance did not occur in a small group.

WHAT YOU MIGHT SEE WHEN GUIDED PRACTICE GOES OFF TRACK

You might see almost no small-group reading instruction in classrooms where guided practice has gone off track. Working in small groups has resumed its rightful role in most primary grade classrooms lately because the trend toward guided reading with those little leveled readers has replaced the basal anthology in many districts. Basal publishers may not have intended for those hefty anthologies to be used with the entire class as whole-class instruction for the duration of the literacy block five days per week. But that's what happened in lots of schools. There was simply so much to teach in the core program that teachers claimed they had no time for anything else.

Even in primary classes, the presence of small-group instruction is not a guarantee that the instruction is worthy. "What's your objective?" I asked a first-grade teacher in a building where I do a lot of coaching.

"Guided reading," she responded somewhat indignantly, as if this should have been obvious. The problem is that guided reading is not an objective; guided reading is an instructional format. Readers are guided most efficiently when there is a specific lesson objective: Identify the problem and the solution in a story; locate words that begin with the "S" sound; figure out the author's message. These are objectives that can be measured at the end of a lesson. Guided practice that goes off track ignores the components of solid literacy instruction and is conducted as if simply meeting with a small group is the whole goal, that whatever occurs during the time the group is together is of negligible consequence. The quality of the instruction is poor.

When I coach in primary classrooms, I often notice that teachers have only a superficial understanding of what their students' instructional levels mean. One group may read at a level sixteen; another at a twenty. "But what skill strengths and deficits do these levels represent?" I ask.

Teachers often have trouble answering this question. Although we have a variety of assessment instruments available for pinpointing students' instructional levels as well as our day-to-day work with students, some teachers do not use this information to plan instruction—to make sure their lessons have objectives matched to what students need most.

Beyond the primary grades, the situation is often even worse. Many intermediate-grade teachers are still stuck in the whole-class-instruction mode and do not even attempt guided practice at the

> Readers are guided most efficiently when there is a specific lesson objective: Identify the problem and the solution in a story; locate words that begin with the "S" sound; figure out the author's message.

small-group level. Everyone reads and discusses the same novel. (Actually, some students do not really read it because it is too difficult for them.) Each day looks a lot like the day before. It's the same routine: Read the chapter, answer a list of questions, discuss the answers. There is no gradual release of responsibility to students. There is no objective beyond absorbing the content of the text, no attempt to help students grow as strategic readers and writers.

In classrooms of all levels, guided practice also can go off track by scheduling small groups only sporadically. I encountered this problem in a district where I was trying hard to help teachers improve test scores. I presented workshops on providing guided practice in small groups. I went into classrooms and modeled lessons that moved from whole class to small group. The building literacy consultant followed up with coaching support. In debriefing sessions, I asked teachers if they were working with small groups.

"Oh, yes," they assured me. I was elated!

But when I asked my next question—"How many groups do you see each day?"—I could see I had gotten excited too soon.

"We have time for only one group most days."

Readers need guided practice with text at their instructional level every day—not from a paraprofessional but from a *teacher* who knows a lot about reading!

At that rate, most students would meet with their small group only one or two times every week. Surely that is not enough to make a difference, especially for struggling readers. Struggling readers need guided practice with text at their instructional level every day—not from a paraprofessional but from a *teacher* who knows a lot about reading!

Note that guided practice means that the teacher is doing the guiding. Some teachers set students to work in literature circles or book clubs and call it *guided practice*. In fact, such activities, though valid pieces of the curriculum, are more appropriately viewed as *independent application* since, for the most part, students engaged in these activities are operating independent of teacher scaffolding.

At the other extreme is the teacher who hovers endlessly at one student's desk, re-teaching the entire lesson because the student (probably before he even got back to his seat) proclaimed, "I don't get it!" Rather than teaching into the first step that the child missed and moving on to the next needy student, the teacher spends seven or eight minutes reviewing *all* of the steps. Meanwhile, everyone else in the class who also wants the teacher's attention waits…and waits… and waits. This should be a clear sign to coaches that guided practice has gone off track because this teacher is doing more to create dependence than independence; some students thrive on this type of private tutorial and are lifetime members of the "I-don't-get-it club."

- How do you identify the students who will work in each of your guided-practice groups?
- How many times per week do you meet with each guided-practice group, and approximately how long is each session?
- How do you determine your objectives for small-group guided practice?
- How do you assure that students are really moving toward independence in guided practice?
- How do you promote active engagement among all students during guided-practice sessions?
- How do you support students who need extra help without creating a sense of dependency?

Independent Practice

TIME FRAME: ABOUT ONE HOUR (OR MORE) CONCURRENTLY WITH GUIDED PRACTICE

We need students who can work and think independently. Sometimes we aren't aware of the real value of this independence (or lack thereof) until students move on to the next grade or the next school. That unhappy teacher moans, "These kids can't do *anything* by themselves. They need someone to hold their hand. They have no idea how to solve their own problems." Without an intentional effort to produce independent learners, teachers will instead produce learners who are *dependent*.

WHAT GOOD TEACHERS DO TO PROVIDE INDEPENDENT PRACTICE

Students need independent practice in all five critical areas of literacy as defined by the Report of the National Reading Panel (2000): phonemic awareness, phonics, fluency, vocabulary, comprehension— plus oral language and writing skills. They also need to do lots of independent reading.

First, coaches will notice that independent practice means lots of independent reading in classrooms that adhere to an explicit literacy teaching model. A chunk of time each day is devoted to students' self-selection of books at a level "just right" for their reading pleasure. That means that they can read the books easily with few or no word-identification issues. They can also readily comprehend those texts.

Good teachers know that students don't always choose books that match their independent reading capacity, so they talk to their students about how to select appropriate books. They understand how to help students find books they can read easily, in genres they prefer, with characters, plots, and themes that will appeal to them. Good teachers will try to read many of the books they make available for independent reading. They give short book talks to their students that describe some of the most salient literary features and entice children to select a particular book.

Coaches also will notice that a good teacher includes student accountability along with student choice: "When you read your independent reading book today, mark two places where you made a personal connection, and be ready to talk about them when we all get back together at the end of the morning."

Or, "Today I want you to choose a nonfiction book and notice at least three details that support the main idea." When children have a purpose for their independent reading, they are more likely to stay focused on their book.

Twenty minutes of independent reading probably is sufficient for intermediate- and upper-grade- students. Primary-grade-children (even kindergarten) should gradually build their stamina for reading independently. Begin with five minutes for the youngest readers and add minutes as children learn to sustain focus.

By the way, coaches need to be aware that the National Reading Panel was inconclusive in its endorsement of independent reading. While it makes perfect sense that consistent reading improves reading performance, there simply weren't enough studies to make this claim conclusively. Independent reading was *associated* with gains in reading scores, but could not be proven to be the *cause* of those gains. This insight is important to coaches and teachers because we want to make sure that children have time to read independently during the school day, but this time should not be a substitute for other important components of reading instruction.

Good teachers also provide students with about another twenty minutes for independent practice with other related literacy components. Good teachers somehow navigate this labyrinth of possibilities and design applications that are not only connected to the text read for whole-class or small-group instruction, but differentiated according to individual student needs. Wow! While this task sounds formidable—and it is—success doesn't hinge on some special talent that a few teachers are born with and others totally lack. Success in this realm comes to those who are willing to take the time to PLAN.

The irony is that the multi-faceted curriculum we create with careful planning is one of the factors that made teaching attractive to most of us in the first place. I was working recently with a team of curriculum writers whose first task was to design the explicit lessons for shared reading and then to develop independent applications integrated with other literacy components.

When children have a purpose for their independent reading, they are more likely to stay focused on their book.

Success in this realm comes to those who are willing to take the time to PLAN.

"This was the fun part, the creative part," they told me afterward. They saw how all of the literacy pieces fit together and how this integration could be made real to students, too.

Coaches will notice right away that teachers who plan for independent literacy applications are typically highly committed to their work since thoughtful planning requires time beyond the school day. Good teachers are willing to put in the extra time and effort because they thrive on the creativity that keeps their minds professionally alert to new possibilities.

And what are the possibilities? The options are endless with entire books devoted to classroom activities in each area. The best we can do here is to identify the areas of comprehensive literacy that teachers should address. That way, when someone asks, "What should the rest of the class do while I'm working with my small group?" the coach will be able to respond knowledgeably. (See the Bibliography at the end of this book for useful resources to support different areas of reading and writing.)

At the primary level, comprehensive literacy should incorporate phonological awareness—the capacity to manipulate sounds—and, beyond that, phonics—matching sounds to letters. Good teachers also recognize the role of fluency. Fluency is manifested in accurate and expressive oral reading with an appropriate pace. But the real reason teachers need to support students' fluency practice is that freedom from word identification problems enhances comprehension. Similarly, continued work with vocabulary improves comprehension as well. And the explicit teaching of comprehension strategies also enhances literacy performance.

Although the National Reading Panel didn't study the impact of oral language development or writing on reading, there is other research evidence that these components, too, should be part of the literacy curriculum. Good teachers weave all of this together in a way that makes sense to their students. It makes sense because Sam and Jackie need to work on their fluency, so they do that while Marcie and Michael are receiving intensive phonics support. Meanwhile, Tamara and Elliot are off to the library to work on an Internet project that integrates math and writing. Another group of five students sits in the corner running their own literature circle to practice comprehension strategies with a text they have selected. Good teachers recognize that differentiated instruction like this is a natural outgrowth of high-quality comprehensive literacy instruction. Good coaches realize that most teachers will not have reached such a level of peak performance yet. But meaningful differentiation is a noble goal and one that a coach and teacher can pursue together.

Good teachers are willing to put in the extra time and effort because they thrive on the creativity that keeps their minds professionally alert to new possibilities.

The real reason teachers need to support students' fluency practice is that freedom from word identification problems enhances comprehension.

WHAT YOU MIGHT SEE IF INDEPENDENT PRACTICE GOES OFF TRACK

There are many tell-tale signs that independent practice—either independent reading or independent skill application—has gone awry. For independent reading, you might notice that there is too much or too little reading taking place. It sounds odd that we would accuse any teacher of too much independent reading in the classroom. However, there are some instructional models that provide children with much time to read at the expense of any (or almost any) explicit instruction. Any direct teaching whatsoever comes in the form of "mini-lessons," during which time the teacher models something quickly and then sends students on their way to try it on their own.

On the flip side, too little independent reading takes place in many classrooms. Unless students are given sufficient time to try out their learning by themselves, without a teacher hovering nearby, we'll never know whether they can manage on their own. We'll never even know whether they can handle a similar reading task in a testing situation. I see this all the time when I'm coaching teachers. The teacher reads a text with her students and discusses it thoroughly. In return, children respond brilliantly on the accompanying written comprehension questions.

"Fabulous!" thinks the teacher. "These kids are prepared for any question that comes their way on a test." Then comes the test—and the test results, which fall far short of the teacher's expectations. The teacher is perplexed and wonders how this could have happened.

It happened in this case because there was a huge gulf for these students between responding to a text that had been *taught* to them and responding to a text that they read *on their own*. This disconnect could have been resolved with more independent reading. Following her initial instruction, if this teacher had given her students a piece of literature comparable to her first text selection and required them to answer the questions without any input from her, the test results wouldn't have been a surprise at all. Moreover, she could have gone back to re-teach points that had caused her students to falter.

Independent reading goes off track when teachers are not familiar with their students and with the books they like to read. A well-read teacher can be quite useful in expanding the reading repertoire of a student by knowing the literature and by tuning in to the students' reading interests and habits.

In the primary grades, it's easy to stay ahead of what kids are reading because the stories are short and teachers can read them quickly. But as soon as texts become longer, it's almost impossible for teachers to keep up. I've been in classrooms where teachers try to bluff their way through a book conference by asking general questions about the characters, problem, or theme. All seems to be going well with the

Unless students are given sufficient time to try out their learning by themselves, without a teacher hovering nearby, we'll never know whether they can manage on their own.

Independent reading goes off track when teachers are not familiar with their students and with the books they like to read.

student responding thoughtfully, giving answers that sound accurate and insightful. Then another student, eavesdropping from elsewhere in the room pipes up: "*That* didn't happen. I read this book, too, and this character never …" It's almost impossible to have a really good conversation about a book you haven't read.

Sometimes the extent or the type of independent-skill application can cause independent practice to go off track. Some teachers scorn any kind of practice material like workbooks, dittos, worksheets, or even the newly coined "think sheets." Likewise, I often refer to the worksheet-type pages I designed for my books *Constructing Meaning through Kid-Friendly Comprehension Strategy Instructions* (Maupin House, 2004) and *Teaching Written Response to Text* (Maupin House, 2001) as "templates," as they are generic forms that can be used with any book.

But here's the reality: kids need practice! How do musicians or sports figures get good at their trade? They practice! Of course readers don't need to complete worksheets to get good at reading, but they need to do *something* to demonstrate mastery! In fact, some of these worksheets (a.k.a. think sheets, forms, and templates) are quite acceptable as a means of monitoring students' reading and writing progress—as long as they don't dominate the curriculum and there is a lot of real reading happening, too.

How plausible is it that all twenty-five students need the same graphic organizer for written response or an identical vocabulary activity? Coaches should be wary of teachers who consistently dole out full-class sets of any skill sheet.

On the other hand, one of the easiest-to-recognize indicators of misguided independent-skill application is when every student in the class is given the *same* worksheet. How plausible is it that all twenty-five students need the same graphic organizer for written response or an identical vocabulary activity? Coaches should be wary of teachers who consistently dole out full-class sets of any skill sheet.

Another clue that independent skill practice is out-of-control is when the teacher staples a bunch of these templates together and hands them to students at the beginning of the morning to keep them busy while she is working with groups. Sometimes the source of these templates is my own *Constructing Meaning* book. Ouch! Sometimes the pages the teacher selects don't even coordinate well with the day's text. Double ouch!

Learning centers also deserve your close scrutiny. If they promote hands-on activities that reinforce curriculum connections, great. But if they are busy-work centers with little significant connection to anything, not so great.

- What kinds of opportunities do you provide for students to apply new skills and strategies to their independent reading and writing?
- How do you differentiate your instruction based on students' individual needs?
- How do you get your students to read and write independently while you work with small groups?
- How do you help your students decide what books are appropriate for independent reading?
- How do you ensure that your students master new skills and strategies to the point of *independence*?
- How much time do you provide for independent reading in your classroom each day and how does this fit into your literacy block?

Reflection

TIME FRAME: FIVE TO TEN MINUTES

Good teachers make sure they set aside time in the literacy block every day to help students reflect on their learning. In fact, reflection may occur at other times during the instructional sequence as well, as teachers move from one instructional component to the next and want to take stock of where their kids are on the learning curve. Be aware that you may see and hear good reflection somewhere other than just at the end of literacy time.

The best learning isn't about what happened in class today; it's about what will happen in class tomorrow. Learning is about transfer: Can students apply what they learned today to what they will do tomorrow and forever afterward? If the answer to that question is *yes*, then solid learning has taken place. If there is no transfer, today's lesson didn't accomplish much. So how do good teachers know if today's learning will transfer? You can't be absolutely certain about transfer until students launch into the next day's work—with more competence than they demonstrated today. However, you can get a "sneak preview" by doing something very simple: asking children to talk about their learning.

WHAT GOOD TEACHERS DO TO HELP STUDENTS REFLECT ON LITERACY LEARNING

Good teachers pose a few basic questions to get the discussion going: What did we do today? What was easy? What was hard? How would you teach this new strategy or skill to someone from our class who was absent today? The answers to these questions will let you know if children are thinking about their thinking and whether they can articulate that thinking. That's metacognition. If they can describe what they learned and recognize what they *think* they understand and what is still confusing to them, that's a useful first step in gauging the learning that took place.

A couple of follow-up questions will tell you whether or not students have a sense of the big picture, how today's lesson fits into the long-range literacy goals: What do you think we should work on tomorrow? How will you be able to use what you learned today as you read and write by yourself?

Good teachers will also invite some students to share examples of what they learned, to be accountable to the specific lesson objective that was set at the beginning of the morning and which was established as a target for today's independent reading. Good teachers might ask all students to share their evidence with a partner but have just a few children address the whole class in order to keep this final part of the lesson short and focused.

WHAT YOU MIGHT SEE WHEN REFLECTION GOES OFF TRACK

In too many classrooms, there is no time set aside for reflection. The literacy block simply ends when time runs out. The teacher looks up at the clock from the table where she is still meeting with a small group: "Oh, my gosh…look at the time. Put your books away and line up for lunch." There is no expectation that anything more final than the ringing of a bell will signal the end of literacy and the transition to the next part of the day.

In other cases, the teacher may plan for a more formal lesson culmination, but the time is spent summing up rather than reflecting—and it's the teacher who does the talking: "Remember when you need to identify the lesson a story teaches, follow these three steps…" While that gives students one more opportunity to review the process and may satisfy the teacher's need for closure, it offers no insight into students' thinking about their thinking and no direction to the teacher as she prepares for tomorrow's instruction.

ASK THE TEACHER:
- How do you bring closure to your literacy block?
- How do you get students to reflect on the progress they made as readers and writers in today's lesson?
- How do you decide where to go next with your literacy instruction?

Study Questions for Chapter Four

1. What kinds of data do we have available to determine how students will be grouped for small-group instruction?

2. (For coaches) How can we help teachers determine the skill/strategy needs of students at different levels?

3. What is standing in the way of making small-group instruction a consistent part of the literacy block for all students every day?

4. How can we get small-group instruction to focus more on "student talk" rather than "teacher talk?"

5. What areas of literacy do teachers need to know more about in order to plan effective activities for students' independent work?

6. What new books at different reading levels can we share with students for independent reading?

7. How are we doing with written response to open-ended comprehension questions? What additional support would be useful to improve students' performance on these questions?

8. How does self-reflection benefit students as literacy learners? How does student reflection benefit teachers? How can we make sure that we devote time to reflection each day?

Part II
Understanding
Coaching

5

When and How to Intervene

I am in and out of schools a lot working with literacy coaches and directly with teachers. While each context is different, the truth is that patterns quickly emerge. Similar instructional issues pop up time after time. It turns out that the hard parts of literacy teaching are difficult not just for beginning teachers, but for teachers with varying years of experience. And the same problems that plague teachers in high-poverty, urban centers also impact instruction in affluent, suburban districts.

In this chapter, I describe some of the recurring problems teachers typically experience and suggest possible interventions to help teachers navigate these challenges. Some interventions lend themselves to a simple dialogue with a teaching colleague to help with professional growth. (Note that the operative word here is *dialogue*. That means that both the coach and the teacher have a voice. This is not a time for the coach to talk and the teacher only to listen.)

Other interventions may be addressed through support right in the classroom. *What* that support may look like in each case—observation of the teacher's instruction, modeling classroom lessons with students while the teacher observes, co-planning, or co-teaching lessons with the teacher—is described on the following pages. I also specify resources found in this book and elsewhere that will be useful as you begin to implement the interventions. You'll find all of this information in the charts that follow to help you make quick decisions about meeting colleagues' needs during your busy day.

Recurring Problems and Suggested Interventions

Problem 1: The teacher does not have a lesson objective, or the objective may be unclear or addressed ineffectively, superficially, or inaccurately.

Teaching without a clear, well-defined objective is an area that coaches should address immediately because it is nearly impossible to teach a good lesson when there is no defined focus. Teachers are sometimes insecure about choosing objectives and do not know how to determine what an appropriate objective might be. Although it would seem that student performance should be the best gauge of which objective to choose, performance alone is not enough to guide some teachers. At times, they need more support in knowing where to look to even *identify* useful objectives for their students.

The teacher does not have a lesson objective, or the objective may be unclear or addressed ineffectively, superficially, or inaccurately.	
Intervention 1	**Help the teacher identify sources of literacy objectives.**
Professional Dialogue	Model the thinking process you use in choosing a literacy objective.
Classroom Support	Select and use an icon students can easily locate in the classroom to identify today's objective.
Resources	State literacy frameworks, district literacy curriculum
Intervention 2	**Help the teacher use available assessment data to determine an appropriate follow-up objective.**
Professional Dialogue	Analyze data with the teacher for strengths and weaknesses: What skill or strategy deficits contributed to a student's level of performance?
Classroom Support	Chart class performance on objectives and track progress through the year.
Resources	Formal assessment data such as state tests and DRA or DIBELS results; informal assessment data such as performance on daily work
Intervention 3	**Help the teacher determine a logical sequence and pace for meeting essential literacy objectives throughout the year.**
Professional Dialogue	Discuss a realistic (month-by-month) plan for meeting state, district, or grade-level goals.
Classroom Support	Post a list of objectives already addressed in the classroom and continue to add to it.
Resources	State literacy frameworks, district literacy curriculum

Intervention 4	**Help the teacher learn how to explain an objective clearly so students will know how to find evidence in a text to meet the objective.**
Professional Dialogue	Discuss what is included in a high-quality explanation.
Classroom Support	Model a lesson in which you explain an objective to students.
Resources	See p. 28, "What good teachers do to explain." See p. 105, **Checklist for Building Literacy Knowledge**.
Intervention 5	**Help the teacher identify appropriate places in a text to model a particular objective.**
Professional Dialogue	Discuss what is involved in good modeling.
Classroom Support	Model a lesson in which you demonstrate how to model an objective.
Resources	See p. 31, "What good teachers do to model." See p. 105, **Checklist for Building Literacy Knowledge**.
Intervention 6	**Help the teacher learn how to reinforce the same objective selected for shared reading in guided and independent reading.**
Professional Dialogue	Discuss ways that the shared reading objective can be differentiated to meet the needs of learners at different levels.
Classroom Support	Model a small-group lesson in which you reinforce the same objective introduced during shared reading. Model classroom strategies for incorporating the shared-reading objective into independent reading.
Resources	See p. 40, "What good teachers do to provide guided practice." See p. 45, "What good teachers do to provide independent practice." See p. 106, **Checklist for Reinforcing Knowledge**.

Problem 2: The teacher doesn't manage time efficiently during the literacy block.

Much too frequently teachers say to me, "We got a late start on literacy this morning, so we didn't get to guided and independent reading." The fact is, they seem to get a late start on literacy almost *every* morning! Since the morning always begins with shared reading, this results in less time available for guided and independent practice. If there is not enough time on task, we should not be surprised when students' reading does not improve. Below are some "time" issues that can derail literacy instruction with some interventions.

The teacher does not manage time efficiently during the literacy block	
Intervention 1	**Help the teacher develop a strategy for beginning literacy instruction on time each day.**
Professional Dialogue	Work with the teacher to create a classroom schedule and to commit to that schedule.
Classroom Support	Use a timer if necessary to adhere to the agreed-upon schedule.
Resources	Inexpensive timer.
Intervention 2	**Help the teacher activate prior knowledge quickly and effectively without listening to endless student connections.**
Professional Dialogue	Work with the teacher to identify alternative strategies for activating prior knowledge (such as turn-and-talk) that do not eat up valuable instructional time.
Classroom Support	Model a shared reading lesson in which you activate prior knowledge quickly and effectively.
Resources	See p. 21, **Activating and Building Background Knowledge.** See p. 104, **Checklist for Setting the Stage for Literacy Learning**.

Intervention 3	Help the teacher establish classroom routines so that students can manage their time independently while the teacher is working with small groups.
Professional Dialogue	Help the teacher establish routines so students will know: Where to get help when they need it What to do when work is completed Where to put completed work
Classroom Support	Model a classroom discussion in which you help students identify routines that will help their classroom run smoothly.
Resources	Chart paper and markers See p. 109, **Classroom Management Checklist.**

Problem 3: The teacher has difficulty selecting texts matched to different objectives.

Most schools have book rooms chock-full of sets of great texts at multiple reading levels, perfect for small-group work. Often there are single copies of picture books or Big Books suitable for shared reading either in the book room or in the school library.

"How do you know which books go with which objectives?" teachers ask. They often ask me which books *I* would choose. While I love talking about books and willingly share my thoughts about texts that *I* have, ultimately, it is not about the books on *my* shelf, but the books already in *your* school or home on *your* shelf.

I acknowledge that matching books to objectives without a strong background in literacy might seem daunting. More than that, choosing books takes time—lots of time. Here are some things coaches can do to support teachers in this area.

The teacher has difficulty selecting texts matched to different objectives.	
Intervention 1	Create a bibliography of picture books for shared reading with possible objective(s) matched to each book.
Professional Dialogue	Model for the teacher your thinking process as you consider different texts for your objective.
Classroom Support	Help the teacher examine classroom books according to objectives each text could address.
Resources	The books in your book room or school library

Intervention 2	**Label texts in your book room that are used for small-group instruction by level and by possible objectives.**
Professional Dialogue	Introduce teachers to new fiction and nonfiction books that could be used for small-group work. Explain how *you* decide if a leveled text is a good match for a particular objective.
Classroom Support	Help the teacher choose books at various levels that can be used with different groups to address the same objective.
Resources	The books in your book room

Problem 4: The teacher does not really engage students during shared reading.

Too many teachers treat shared reading as a read-aloud. They begin on the first page and read straight through to the end, barely stopping to take a breath, let alone share the experience or think aloud with their students. Shared reading should be interactive. It should be a time for teachers to model their thinking, and for students to begin to apply these same thinking processes. The following suggestions will help coaches intervene to make shared reading more productive.

The teacher does not really engage students during shared reading.	
Intervention 1	**Help the teacher develop techniques for keeping students engaged, even when the teacher is reading aloud and students are primarily listening.**
Professional Dialogue	Brainstorm with the teacher some strategies for keeping students engaged during shared reading (other than round-robin reading).
Classroom Support	Model a shared-reading lesson in which you help students tune in to the text as you model your thinking and elicit their participation.
Resources	See p. 31, "What good teachers do to model" and p. 33, "What good teachers do to bridge." See p. 105, **Checklist for Building Literacy Knowledge**.

Intervention 2	Help the teacher learn how to scaffold the gradual release of responsibility to students during shared reading.
Professional Dialogue	Show the teacher the model of explicit instruction and explain the gradual release of responsibility.
Classroom Support	Model a shared-reading lesson in which you clearly release responsibility as you move from modeling to bridging.
Resources	See p. xii, "Model of Explicit Instruction (Gradual Release of Responsibility)."

Problem 5: The teacher does not meet with small groups consistently, or the small-group instruction is ineffective.

I often feel that this is the single most debilitating problem in literacy instruction today. The consequences of poor-quality small-group instruction (or none at all!) are profound. Here is what I tell teachers: No one actually learns to *read* during shared reading; they learn to *think*. Shared reading supports students when the learning is transferred to text that students can actually *read*; that occurs in guided and independent reading.

This is a worthy battle for all coaches to fight because without excellent small-group instruction, readers will not make the progress they are capable of making, and test scores (yes, those state achievement scores) will be lower than they should be. Try some of these suggestions to move small-group instruction forward in your school.

The teacher does not meet with small groups consistently, or the small-group instruction is ineffective.	
Intervention 1	Help the teacher group students according to available data.
Professional Dialogue	A discussion about grouping should focus not only on *level*, but on *skill* and *strategy* needs.
Classroom Support	Observe groupings of students to evaluate the appropriateness of the levels as well as the inter-dynamics of group members.
Resources	Formal assessment data such as state tests and DRA/DIBELS scores and informal data such as classroom work

Intervention 2	**Help the teacher establish groups early in the year. (Do not let him postpone this due to insufficient assessment data.)**
Professional Dialogue	Talk with the teacher about how students can best be grouped so that there are a reasonable number of groups and children placed appropriately.
Classroom Support	Visit the classroom during small-group instruction to determine whether students are grouped appropriately.
Resources	Student work samples, available assessment data, input from previous year's teacher if available
Intervention 3	**Help the teacher identify objectives for small-group instruction beyond those assessed on the state achievement test.**
Professional Dialogue	Discuss objectives within multiple dimensions of literacy: phonemic awareness, phonics, fluency, vocabulary, comprehension, oral language, and writing.
Classroom Support	Help the teacher complete a planning sheet specifying how many times per week a group will focus on a particular area of literacy.
Resources	A list of grade-level expectations in various areas of literacy as specified on district or state literacy frameworks
Intervention 4	**Help teachers understand that the traditional model of "guided reading" in primary grades may not provide enough focus on clear objectives to advance students' literacy skills.**
Professional Dialogue	Discuss with teachers how to support readers before, during, and after reading during a small-group lesson that focuses on a specific objective. (Most of the small-group lesson is devoted to practice rather than explaining and modeling.)
Classroom Support	Model a small-group lesson demonstrating the emphasis on *practicing* the identified skill or strategy.
Resources	Developmentally appropriate text for students in the demonstration group

Intervention 5	Help the teacher structure the literacy block to facilitate meeting with at least three small groups per day.
Professional Dialogue	Create with the teacher a realistic, weekly small-group rotation sheet.
Classroom Support	Model the orchestration of three reading groups within one literacy block in a classroom.
Resources	Texts and other support materials for three literacy groups

Problem 6: The teacher does not provide students with meaningful independent work.

The days of fill-in-the-blank literacy exercises should be long gone. Teachers who are having trouble coming up with authentic forms of literacy practice need help from a coach who can assist them in designing worthwhile independent tasks.

The teacher does not provide students with meaningful independent work.	
Intervention 1	Help the teacher identify and plan for tasks that are authentic reading and writing applications that reinforce skills and strategies students really need.
Professional Dialogue	Talk with the teacher about what makes a literacy activity "authentic," not "busy work" (a task that can be applied *beyond* the classroom rather than just *in* the classroom).
Classroom Support	Share specific activities that you have tried and used successfully with students; introduce some of these activities in the teacher's classroom.
Resources	Create a resource for teachers in your building with generic activities in different areas of literacy.

Intervention 2	**Help the teacher identify and plan for differentiated reinforcement applications according to students' performance levels (different students doing different activities).**
Professional Dialogue	Talk with the teacher about how to modify a particular task for readers of different levels.
Classroom Support	Model in a classroom how you would introduce one basic activity differentiated for students at three different learning levels.
Resources	See the Bibliography for suggested books on differentiated instruction.
Intervention 3	**Help the teacher develop a management plan for making independent work time truly independent without excessive student interruptions.**
Professional Dialogue	Talk with the teacher about what is getting in the way of student productivity during independent work time and help him address these issues systematically.
Classroom Support	Model a conversation in a classroom where you and the students establish routines for independent work time; make a chart specifying these routines.
Resources	Chart paper, markers

Problem 7: The teacher does not provide students with sufficient time for independent reading or the independent reading time is not productive.

Too often, independent reading is the last item on the morning agenda. The basic message is, "If you finish all of your other work, then you can read." In fact, independent reading should be the *first* item on the list. Although we can't count on independent reading to build skills and strategies, this daily encounter with easy-to-read text builds stamina, fluency, and hopefully a love of reading. There are several ways a coach can serve teachers in making independent reading a more integral part of classroom literacy.

	The teacher does not provide students with sufficient time for independent reading or the independent reading time is not productive.
Intervention 1	**Help the teacher develop a plan to incorporate independent reading into the daily literacy block so that it is more than "something to do when all of your other work is finished."**
Professional Dialogue	Decide how many minutes would be optimal for students to read independently (based on grade level and prior experience with independent reading); decide when during the literacy block students will read.
Classroom Support	Model a conversation in a classroom where you establish routines for independent reading behaviors; make a chart describing these behaviors.
Resources	Chart paper, markers
Intervention 2	**Help the teacher develop ways to make students accountable for their independent reading by meeting a specified objective.**
Professional Dialogue	Talk with the teacher about *why* most students need some form of accountability during independent reading (keeps them focused); determine simple techniques for holding students accountable (i.e., using sticky notes to mark applications of a particular strategy).
Classroom Support	Model a demonstration lesson in which you monitor your reading with the use of sticky notes or other techniques. Model a reflecting session in which you ask students to share strategy applications from their independent reading.
Resources	Sticky notes and Independent reading books

Intervention 3	Help the teacher develop criteria for selecting "just right" books to share with students.
Professional Dialogue	Talk with teacher about what might make a book a good selection for independent reading at this grade level.
Classroom Support	Model a classroom discussion in which you ask students to tell you what makes a book "just right" for them (criteria will vary); create a chart with criteria listed.
Resources	Chart paper, markers
Intervention 4	Help the teacher learn how to introduce new books with a brief "book chat" that motivates students to want to read a particular book.
Professional Dialogue	Talk with the teacher about the value of reading at least some of the books in the classroom library. Discuss ways to talk about new books that will entice students to read them.
Classroom Support	Model a "book chat" in which students are introduced to a few new books. Say just enough to pique their interest and explain who might find this book "just right" based on level and interest.
Resources	A few independent reading books from classroom or school library
Intervention 5	Help the teacher organize the classroom library so it is student friendly.
Professional Dialogue	Talk with the teacher about different ways to organize books in the classroom library (e.g., by genre, level, author, topic, etc.).
Classroom Support	Assist the teacher in organizing the classroom library, making it attractive and manageable for students.
Resources	Book bins, labels for book bins

Problem 8: The teacher does not have identified criteria like rubrics or criteria charts with which to evaluate students' work.

There is a lack of criteria in many classrooms upon which instructional decisions are made. For example, students have to write responses to comprehension questions that require them to make personal connections to text. What does a good response to such a question look like in first grade? What does it look like in fourth grade or sixth grade?

With clearer expectations, teachers can evaluate students' performance more accurately. They can also provide better explanations to students *before* they engage in a task which would increase their likelihood of success the first time around. This is a fairly easy issue for coaches to address, although the same process will need to be applied several times to establish criteria for different tasks.

The teacher does not have identified criteria like rubrics or criteria charts with which to evaluate students' work.	
Intervention 1	**Help the teacher identify necessary criteria for mastering specific objectives.**
Professional Dialogue	Talk with the teacher about what counts as success in meeting the standards of different reading and writing tasks (e.g., narrative writing, fluency, responses to open-ended comprehension questions, etc.); identify three or four basic criteria for each task.
Classroom Support	Work alongside the teacher to assess student work samples according to the established criteria.
Resources	State-generated rubrics to assess students' reading and writing performance on state-tested tasks See the Bibliography for resources on comprehension and criteria for responding to open-ended comprehension questions.

Intervention 2	Help the teacher to state criteria in language that students at his grade level can understand.
Professional Dialogue	Talk with the teacher about how to describe the criteria for meeting a particular objective in language that students in this grade can understand.
Classroom Support	Provide an opportunity—perhaps during a grade-level or faculty meeting—for the teacher to create a criteria chart in grade-appropriate language to be posted in the classroom. Model a session in which you introduce the criteria for a task to students and help students reflect on their own performance based on this criteria.
Resources	Chart paper and markers

Problem 9: The teacher has not created a classroom environment that supports literacy.

All children have a right to a school environment that is clean and safe and facilitates the work that takes place there. Sometimes there is too much focus on the classroom environment, and other times there is not enough.

Below are some of the most persistent issues I see as I am in and out of classrooms which would benefit from a little hands-on attention from a caring coach.

The teacher has not created a classroom environment that supports literacy.	
Intervention 1	Help the teacher recognize that clutter does not contribute to students' learning and could be discarded, trimmed, or reorganized.
Professional Dialogue	Talk with the teacher about strategies for deciding what stays and what goes—and how to manage and file what stays.
Classroom Support	Work alongside the teacher to sort and throw out.
Resources	Folders, file boxes, trash bags

Intervention 2	**Help the teacher recognize that more visual appeal based on authentic classroom activities would make the classroom environment a more dynamic place to learn.**
Professional Dialogue	Talk with the teacher about simple ways to use student work, rubrics, and other instructional charts and graphics to add color and interest to the classroom.
Classroom Support	Accompany the teacher to visit other classrooms with a well-designed (but realistic) classroom environment. Work alongside the teacher to redo bulletin boards and wall displays.
Resources	Student writing, criteria charts, student-created graphics
Intervention 3	**Help the teacher decide how to configure the arrangement of furniture for maximum usefulness.**
Professional Dialogue	Talk with the teacher about how students use space throughout the literacy block. Devise a plan together that allows *all* parts of the classroom to serve students' literacy needs.
Classroom Support	After furniture has been rearranged, visit the classroom to provide the teacher with feedback about how well the configuration is meeting the teacher's and students' needs.
Resources	See p. 108, **Classroom Environment Checklist**.
Intervention 4	**Help the teacher reorganize and enhance the classroom library.**
Professional Dialogue	Talk with the teacher about ways to organize texts according to level, genre, author, topic, etc. so that they are attractively displayed and accessible to students.
Classroom Support	Work alongside the teacher to redo the classroom library.
Resources	Book bins, labels, bookcases Many communities now have recycled books suitable for classroom libraries available to teachers for free.

With so much emphasis on state assessments, many teachers (upon the insistence of their district) spend a huge amount of time teaching to objectives that are tested. These areas are typically reading comprehension and writing to a prompt related to a specific writing genre such as narrative, expository, or descriptive writing.

The reason that students perform poorly on these tests often has less to do with the tested objective—inferring text meaning, for example, in reading comprehension—than with the foundational skills that ultimately make it possible for a student to make an inference: word identification, fluency, vocabulary knowledge, basic construction of meaning.

Unfortunately, in their zeal to improve test scores, teachers sometimes do not address these underlying skills. Some of the omissions I note most frequently are:

- lack of attention to decoding and sight words beyond the primary grades for students with obvious deficits in these areas
- too little attention to vocabulary at all grade levels
- fluency instruction that is still stuck in "round-robin" mode despite tons of research evidence that this is bad practice
- comprehension strategy instruction that is superficial
- scant focus on oral language development, including a lack of meaningful discussions about text, along with an over-emphasis on written response

Coaches need to help teachers tune in to what students really need! This means on some occasions that they must move out of their own comfort zone. As a coach, you may be really strong in primary-grade phonics, but if you have a fourth-grade teacher who is struggling with fluency instruction, it is up to you to support that need.

The teacher does not attend to one or more critical areas of literacy (phonemic awareness, phonics, fluency, vocabulary, comprehension, oral language, writing), despite students' needs.

Intervention 1	**Help the teacher clarify grade-level expectations for students in all areas of literacy so she will know when student performance is below standard.**
Professional Dialogue	Talk with the teacher about what skills students should have in each area of literacy in order to identify whether students are achieving these benchmarks.
Classroom Support	Observe students as they engage in literacy tasks, and help the teacher determine the underlying reason for a student's poor performance (e.g., does poor comprehension signal a lack of comprehension strategies or an inability to decode words?).
Resources	State or district documents with benchmarks for all components of literacy
Intervention 2	**Help the teacher identify materials and techniques for teaching components of literacy with which he may not be sufficiently knowledgeable.**
Professional Dialogue	Ask the teacher which areas of literacy instruction might benefit from some additional input from you. What kinds of input would be most helpful?
Classroom Support	Create packets of generic activities that teachers can use at a particular grade level for instruction and reinforcement of different literacy areas. For example: a few activities for building fluency and some ideas to extend writing.
Resources	See p. 101, **Literacy Needs Assessment**. Check out websites for sight words, fluency, etc; many have fabulous, free resources.

Problem 11: The teacher does not assess students' progress in literacy, or students do not seem to be making progress.

In some ways, we seem to assess students too much; in other circumstances, there may not be enough assessment. But like the previous problem (lack of attention to students' *real* literacy needs), assessing a prerequisite skill can determine if that is the underlying cause of the problem. In the wake of those mandatory, annual state tests come many look-alike instruments fashioned by individual districts to mimic the content and format of the "real" test. Districts want a "heads-up" on how their students are doing and the chance to re-teach objectives where students may be faltering.

The issue is, however, that when we get the scores back and they are low, teachers re-double their efforts on the objective where students performed poorly, re-teaching and retesting. Coaches need to help teachers see beneath the surface of an assessment to determine what else might need to be evaluated.

The teacher does not assess students' progress in literacy, or students do not seem to be making progress.	
Intervention 1	**Help the teacher identify ways to assess students' performance in multiple areas of literacy informally through classroom work.**
Professional Dialogue	Brainstorm with the teacher about what might account for a student's low performance in a particular area of literacy.
Classroom Support	Work alongside the teacher to evaluate student work samples to analyze the cause of low performance.
Resources	Student work samples in reading and writing
Intervention 2	**Help the teacher find test-length passages to assess different literacy objectives.**
Professional Dialogue	Talk with the teacher about the difference between testing students on passages that have been *taught* and passages that they are reading for the first time in a testing situation (a "cold read").
Classroom Support	Observe students as they are tested on different literacy objectives to try to determine whether the instruction that preceded the assessment was adequate.
Resources	Previous test passages released by your state or other states, often available on the website with state assessment information; short texts of about the same length as test passages

Intervention 3	Help the teacher scaffold the teaching of individual objectives leading to independence so that students will perform optimally on assessments.
Professional Dialogue	Talk with the teacher about steps necessary to move students toward independence in meeting an objective.
Classroom Support	Model and coach a series of classroom lessons that include diminishing amounts of explaining, modeling, bridging, and guided practice as students work toward independence.
Resources	See p. xii, "Model of Explicit Instruction (Gradual Release of Responsibility)."

Problem 12: The teacher does not engage students in high-level talk about text.

Teachers often bemoan students' lack of critical thinking about the texts they read. Sometimes, however, students are not given opportunities to develop their higher-level thought processes. With a rush to get answers down on paper, the dialogue that would push students to think beyond basic text elements is all but ignored.

Developing the power of students' thinking is an area that probably deserves attention by *all* coaches for at least some of the teachers in your building.

The teacher does not engage students in high-level talk about text.	
Intervention 1	Help the teacher identify qualities of a good discussion and instructional techniques for achieving those qualities.
Professional Dialogue	Talk with the teacher about how to get students actively engaged in discussions that generate enthusiasm about their reading and lead to critical thinking about a text.
Classroom Support	Accompany the teacher to a classroom where a colleague leads engaging discussions about literature; debrief with the teacher about what was observed. Model a lesson in which students move from literal understanding of a text to more critical thinking.
Resources	Question stems that generate thinking at different levels, such as those related to Bloom's taxonomy or those proposed by your state assessment.

Intervention 2	**Help the teacher develop a system for using comprehension strategies to encourage students to construct their own meaning without answering lists of questions posed by the teacher.**
Professional Dialogue	Talk with the teacher about comprehension strategies and how to get students to actively use them during small-group instruction.
Classroom Support	Accompany the teacher to a classroom where a colleague uses the comprehension strategies meaningfully; debrief with the teacher about what was observed. Model a lesson in which students use the repertoire of comprehension strategies.
Resources	See the Bibliography for resources on comprehension strategies.
Intervention 3	**Help the teacher recognize that discussing answers to questions orally before students write their responses will produce richer responses.**
Professional Dialogue	Discuss with the teacher the kinds of problems struggling students demonstrate in written responses (organization, elaboration, sentence structure, using full sentences, etc,); show the teacher how many of these deficits can be resolved as children experiment with thinking out loud before writing.
Classroom Support	Model a discussion about a text in which you teach students how to structure a well-organized, elaborated response to a comprehension question.
Resources	Use answer organizers and frames; see the Bibliography.
Intervention 4	**Help the teacher identify higher-level questions about text that he may not be asking students frequently enough.**
Professional Dialogue	Examine with the teacher higher-level thinking questions, and consider which are often omitted from discussion.
Classroom Support	Help the teacher write lesson plans for shared reading and small-group instruction that include some of these frequently omitted questions.
Resources	See the Bibliography.

Intervention 5	Help the teacher identify academic language (words to describe character traits, test-question vocabulary, etc.) that helps students talk about their reading meaningfully.
Professional Dialogue	Help the teacher analyze literacy objectives to identify words or concepts that may get in the way of students responding with specific, precise language.
Classroom Support	Help the teacher create word walls with academic language, such as words to describe feelings, transition words, sentence starters, etc.
Resources	District or state literacy objectives

Problem 13: The teacher does not provide students with the opportunity to reflect on their literacy learning.

This problem is everywhere! Teachers almost universally run out of time before pulling students back together to reflect on what they have learned on a particular morning that will help them improve as readers and writers. Or maybe teachers don't even realize they should be encouraging such reflection.

Coaching should contribute to teachers' and students' improved reflection on literacy learning in two important ways: scheduling time for reflection and using that time productively.

The teacher does not provide students with the opportunity to reflect on their literacy learning.

Intervention 1	Help the teacher find instructional time for reflecting on literacy learning each day.
Professional Dialogue	Talk with the teacher about the role of reflecting and assist her in planning for this daily in the literacy block. (Figure out how to shave a few minutes from other areas of literacy instruction to provide reflection time.)
Classroom Support	Include "reflection" on the classroom schedule each day.
Resources	Classroom schedule written on white board or chalkboard

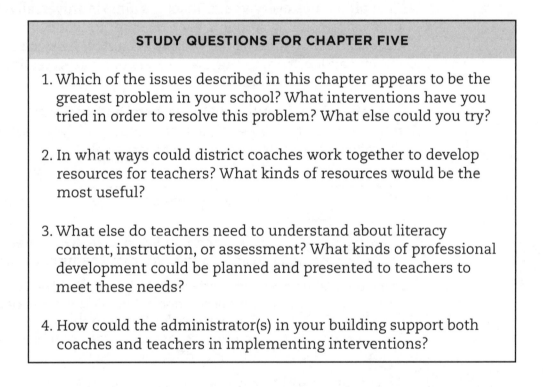

Intervention 2	Help the teacher develop prompts to help students reflect on their literacy learning.
Professional Dialogue	Talk with the teacher about the difference between the *teacher* summing up the learning and the *students* doing their own self-reflection.
Classroom Support	Accompany the teacher to a classroom where children are engaged in self-reflection about their learning; debrief with teacher about observations. Model a 5 – to 10-minute segment in which you help students reflect on what they learned that day as readers and writers along with the logical next step in their literacy learning.
Resources	See the Bibliography.

STUDY QUESTIONS FOR CHAPTER FIVE

1. Which of the issues described in this chapter appears to be the greatest problem in your school? What interventions have you tried in order to resolve this problem? What else could you try?

2. In what ways could district coaches work together to develop resources for teachers? What kinds of resources would be the most useful?

3. What else do teachers need to understand about literacy content, instruction, or assessment? What kinds of professional development could be planned and presented to teachers to meet these needs?

4. How could the administrator(s) in your building support both coaches and teachers in implementing interventions?

6

The Coach/Teacher Dynamic

What Makes a Good Coach Good?

You can find books about coaching with long lists of traits considered essential to becoming an effective coach. I consider five factors especially important:

• Superior knowledge of principles of literacy teaching and learning
• Recognized excellence as an instructor of literacy
• Interest in leading adults
• Ability to raise a teacher's sense of self-efficacy
• Adapting the coaching style to the teaching style

SUPERIOR KNOWLEDGE OF PRINCIPLES OF LITERACY TEACHING AND LEARNING

Many resources on coaching place little value on a coach's actual content knowledge, yet without a strong understanding of literacy—or any academic discipline—coaching cannot make a real difference in a teacher's instructional practices.

Here is an example of the kind of dead end a coach reaches when she does not have a solid grounding in literacy:

The coach asks, "How's it going?"

The teacher responds, "Not very well."

The coach follows up with another generic question like, "What makes you say that?"

The teacher replies, "We just got the scores back from our district assessments, and most of my students are still scoring in the lowest category."

Then there is an uncomfortable silence while the coach tries to figure out what to say next. She offers to look at the scores with the teacher the next day, but this meeting produces little in the way of possible solutions. The coach understands the district assessments but, without a strong foundation in literacy, she is at a loss as to how to interpret them in light of follow-up strategies. In the end, the coach recommends that this teacher speak to her grade-level partner whose students showed significant improvement on this same assessment. "Find out what she did to improve *her* scores," the coach suggests.

When you think about it, the coach didn't make much of a difference here. Her only piece of advice was for the teacher to collaborate with her teaching partner. The teacher could have figured out that much on *her* own!

Consider how differently this entire scenario might have played out with a coach knowledgeable about literacy. When she sat with the teacher to reflect on those low scores, she would have had specific suggestions: "Oh, I see that 'Inferences and Interpretations' are really troublesome for your students. Unfortunately we don't get back data that breaks this down for us and tells us the particular objectives where students are failing. Tomorrow let's look at some of your students' written responses and see which questions are hardest. Then I can come to your room and model some strategies to improve their answers. I'll stick around until you can implement those strategies, too."

The teacher looks relieved. She and the coach agree to look at student work during tomorrow's planning time.

Here is a coach who is making a difference! She will continue to make a difference, not just because she understands the process of coaching but because she understands literacy. This command of content knowledge allows her to "go deep" with the teachers she coaches.

What's on the "short list" of literacy content for coaches to master? I would include:

• The five literacy pillars as defined by the National Reading Panel: phonemic awareness, phonics, fluency, vocabulary, comprehension
• Oral language development
• Shared, guided, and independent reading
• Literacy assessment
• Writing
• English Language Learners
• Learners with special needs—including gifted learners
• Children's literature
• Resources for teaching literacy, including technology
• Content-area literacy
• Literacy needs at different grade levels

There are scores of journals and resource books available to support coaches who need to brush up on one or more of these areas of literacy. Several books are listed in the Bibliography under each category.

RECOGNIZED EXCELLENCE AS AN INSTRUCTOR OF LITERACY

Closely related to literacy content knowledge, coaches must be recognized as excellent teachers of literacy in their own right. If teachers see that you are the kind of educator who achieves results with students, they will be much more likely to follow your lead.

For coaches who have transitioned from classroom teacher to coach in their same school, this is less of a problem. You are a known quantity. Your colleagues may have watched you work with students at various grade levels for years and are fully aware of your excellent track record.

But when a coach comes to a building with no prior history in that school, the situation is different. You may be good at talking the talk. Still, actions speak louder than words. That is why I believe that a coach's day should never be filled entirely with coaching. There should always be some room in the schedule for direct work with children.

Even coaches who have previously taught in a building will find that their credibility wanes after a while if they don't have ongoing "kid-contact." That's what keeps us current—and humble! It's too easy to lose touch with how tough it is to teach a child something really basic like letter sounds or more complex like the skill of summarizing text—unless you are the person responsible for that learning. Hence, coaches who wish to sustain their reputation as excellent coaches will also maintain a day-to-day presence in the learning lives of children.

So how should coaches divide their time? After watching the way this happens in different schools, I think the most realistic plan is for coaches to work with students for about one hour per day—preferably in the afternoon. This keeps the morning open for coaching in the classroom during the literacy block. During that afternoon hour, coaches can see two groups of students for supplementary instruction, not for the entire year but for short-term targeted interventions.

INTEREST IN LEADING ADULTS

The third essential coach characteristic, interest in leading adults, is difficult to predetermine because most new coaches have not worked directly with adults before assuming their coach role. Even if coaches come to their position with superior knowledge of literacy and recognized excellence as teachers of literacy, their excellence was probably established *in* the classroom rather than beyond it.

Sometimes you just can't tell how this is going to play out. Let's be honest here. None of us became teachers because we couldn't wait

> If teachers see that you are the kind of educator who achieves results with students, they will be much more likely to follow your lead.

> I believe that a coach's day should never be filled entirely with coaching. There should always be some room in the schedule for direct work with children.

to work with adults, especially our cranky fourth-grade teacher who didn't teach reading very well. We got into this work because we love kids!

Somewhere along the way, you may have acquired a graduate degree in reading or someone you respect told you that you are an awesome teacher of literacy and you really should share your talents with other teachers. You may have become a coach, not because you were tired of the classroom or eager to get on with your career but out of a sense of loyalty to your profession: This is a way you could give back to the field that you have found so personally rewarding.

Some coaches thrive in their coach position. They love working with multiple teachers at one time and somehow navigate all of the little personal quirks that make professional learning communities interesting—and frustrating. They don't mind stepping into classrooms to teach lessons to students they've never met before. They don't seem to mind that their relationship with the former teacher-next-door has been changed ever so subtly since they are no a longer classroom teacher (but not an administrator, either). They rise to the challenge of beginning again to fashion a new professional identity.

For other coaches who bring equally strong skills to their new role, this simply is not a good fit. They have the expertise, but leading beyond the classroom doesn't feel quite right, not now anyway.

"Why don't I like this?" one of my former graduate students asked me tearfully. She had desperately wanted a position as a literacy coach, and obtained one in a district where the coaching model was operating effectively. Now she was having second thoughts, felt that she had let me down, and wondered what was wrong with her that she was not enthralled with her work as a coach.

As we talked, it became obvious that she simply missed the close relationship she had had with her "own" third graders. This business of working with adults was a chore, not a passion. "Here's a little secret," I confided. "I wasn't ready to be a literacy coach for a very long time. I loved being in the classroom so much that I couldn't imagine a day without kids in it in a significant way."

I stayed in the classroom for twenty-five years, and I don't consider even one of those days time ill-spent. Now when I talk with a teacher about a student who is struggling or obstinate, I can honestly say, "I've met this kid before, and here's what worked for me."

I have counseled several coaches over the past few years who have elected to return to the classroom because at this moment they are better equipped to lead students rather than teachers. And that's okay. In fact, that's great! We need to get past the notion that moving forward as educators means leaving the classroom. What better place to serve education than right next to a child?

As a teacher in a university program that prepares literacy leaders and as a consultant to many districts, working with literacy coaches, I wish I could say there are fail-safe signs that help me identify who will thrive in the role of literacy leader and who will not. My best advice is: Don't push! There is an overwhelming shortage of literacy coaches, to the extent that districts actually "steal" them from each other. It is tempting to push my very qualified candidates into these roles because I know they "have what it takes" to do the job well. But potential coaches need to listen to their heart and move into this role when the time is right for them.

ABILITY TO RAISE A TEACHER'S SENSE OF SELF-EFFICACY

Self-efficacy is the capacity to achieve goals beyond what you, as an individual, thought were realistic or possible. It's that, "Oh, wow!" feeling you get when you accomplish something you never thought was within your grasp. You feel good about yourself! If a coach can help that happen for a teacher, the coach (and the coaching) will be well received.

The capacity to raise a teacher's sense of self-efficacy is not a characteristic of coaches that is typically identified in resources about coaching. More commonly, the essential attribute is regarded as "trust." On closer examination, however, trust is the result of a good coaching relationship. It is earned over time.

How does a coach promote self-efficacy? First, the coach honors the experience and expertise that a teacher brings to the table. Whether a teacher has been teaching for three weeks or thirty years, no one wants to hear, "Throw out everything you thought you knew about teaching reading; let's start over."

Teachers are more receptive to a message that conveys that they are "this close" to excellence: "You are doing so many things right. Let's try this one small change and see if that makes the needed difference in helping your students meet success." You aren't suggesting massive reorganization, just one small modification. If you can make that change seem easy, as well, you will get even more buy-in.

Facilitating self-efficacy means that you leave teachers' dignity intact. You do not betray them in a way that is hurtful or punitive. This raises the whole issue of confidentiality: How much confidentiality is crucial or desirable in a coaching relationship?

I ask this question frequently in coaching seminars, and the words are barely out of my mouth when several hands fly into the air. "You should never, under any circumstance, share what happens in a coaching session with an administrator," some coaches are quick to

---

Facilitating self-efficacy means that you leave teachers' dignity intact. You do not betray them in a way that is hurtful or punitive.

respond. This basic mindset—what happens in Vegas stays in Vegas—is a popular stance with some coaches and they argue the point vehemently.

But after this initial, impassioned response, other voices tentatively come forward with a different message. As one coach told a seminar group recently, "I coach teachers in my building based on the recommendation of my principal. As soon as I leave that classroom, the principal asks, 'How did it go?'"

I listen with interest to these opposing points of view before adding my own voice to the conversation. "Are we all on the same team here?" I ask. "I would prefer to think that the principal is not the enemy, that we are all working together to achieve the same goal: improved learning for students." I also point out that coaches who complain to me that they do not receive adequate support from their administrators are some of the same ones who do not want to include their principal in debriefing sessions about their coaching experiences. But you need to tread carefully!

Here's my solution: All of the stake-holders—principal, coach, teacher, and (when relevant) outside consultant (me)—sit together after a classroom coaching experience to discuss what occurred. That way, everyone hears the message at the same time, in the same way. This also communicates to the teacher that this coaching business is important enough to warrant the administrator's time and attention.

I frame the discussion in a positive way, focusing on what occurred in the lesson, not my evaluation of it. Most often, as we talk together, the teacher is able ultimately to evaluate her own lesson: "Here's why this happened." Or, "Next time I teach this lesson I will be sure to…" Discovering that the solutions to problems were within you from the start, not implanted from outside, is what self-efficacy is all about.

We conclude our meeting with some next steps: "Here are a couple of things that Deirdre might want to work on next that could make a big difference to literacy in her classroom."

This sounds much better than, "Here are some things that Deirdre messed up that she needs to fix…" When we part, everyone, not just Deirdre, has an "assignment." How will the coach support Deirdre? What will the principal do to support her? (See "Protocol for Coach's Observation and Conferring" in **Chapter Seven** to use during debriefing sessions.)

I don't even want to think about how ugly the repercussions can be when conversations around a coaching event occur separately. (Unfortunately, I speak from experience.) The coach talks to the teacher. The coach talks to the administrator. Then, ultimately, the administrator talks to the teacher. Although there may be no malicious intent, words get twisted, taken out of context, and misrepresented. When all is said and done, there are numerous battle scars and all hopes for self-efficacy have been dashed at least for the moment.

ADAPTING THE COACHING STYLE TO THE TEACHING STYLE

Children, even kindergarten students and first graders, are hardly a "blank slate." They come to us with prior experiences, both positive and negative, that shape their experiences as learners. So, too, teachers come to their positions with a history of attitudes and dispositions as well as personal and professional agendas that contribute to the way they do their job. As coaches we sometimes forget that. We forget that all teachers will never be equally committed to best practices, equally capable of applying new professional learning, or equally open to change.

I have grouped teachers into four basic types defined below. These are generalities based on characteristics that apply *most* of the time. Of course there will be many teachers who exhibit behaviors in more than one category. There may be teachers who appear to fall into one category this week and another category next week. Still, coaches tell me that they have met, over and over, the teachers I describe in the four categories below.

Understanding where teachers "are coming from" can help coaches approach them with more realistic expectations and can provide a starting point as to how to best serve their needs. It can also help coaches determine where their time will be spent most productively. The four teacher-types are:

- Three-E teachers: excellent, enthusiastic, energetic
- Three-T teachers: trying hard, timid, too stressed
- Three-O teachers: ornery, outspoken, overbearing
- Three-D teachers: dull, defeated, DONE

THE THREE Es—EXCELLENT, ENTHUSIASTIC, ENERGETIC

Three-E teachers are your greatest asset. These are the teachers who bound into school each morning, eager to try the new strategy you shared with them yesterday. They actually ask *you* about professional articles on subjects that inspire them and practically beg you to come to their classroom to offer insights and feedback on their instruction. They willingly stay after school to plan the next day's literacy lessons and collaborate with the media specialist, music teacher, and other personnel to provide differentiated instruction for the different learners in their classrooms. These teachers may be novice or veteran, and while they may not be excellent just yet, the potential for excellence is there.

As a coach, it might look like there's little you can do for these energetic, enthusiastic teachers who strive to excel. In fact, there's much you can do. First, contribute to their professional passion. Share with them the insights you have gained from your professional reading or conferences and meetings you have attended. Let them borrow your books and journals, and arrange for them to attend professional-development sessions on topics that they care about.

Most literacy coaches don't have a classroom of their own where they can bring other teachers to see best practices in action. Hence, you need to identify classrooms where good things are happening, so teachers who are having difficulty in a particular area can visit and get ideas to bring back to their own room. Three-E teachers are the most likely candidates for becoming classroom models early on.

But coaches, beware! Other teachers in a building will only resent these very good teachers if they are constantly held up as the gold standard. Ultimately, you need to find something to celebrate in many classrooms and invite teachers to those classrooms as well. Remember, teachers don't have to be great at everything to model a best practice; they only need to be good at something. Perhaps there is a teacher who has a great system for classroom management during independent work time. Maybe you have a teacher who works oral language development into her kindergarten curriculum in a seamless manner. Good coaches are in and out of classrooms so often that they catch these "moments of brilliance" and find a way to turn many teachers into instructional models for something.

You may have to mediate between these teachers and the rest of your staff for other reasons as well. Teachers often view Three-E teachers as overachievers, motivated by a desire to please their administrator, no matter what. Sometimes excellence in schools is not rewarded as commonly as fitting in with the majority, even when the majority is all too "average."

In that regard, the coach also needs to make sure that Three-E teachers don't burn themselves out in their zeal to achieve high standards. These are the teachers who volunteer to serve on countless committees, who agree to mentor new teachers to their building, and who are the last to leave school at night and the first to arrive in the morning. Sometimes coaches need to save these teachers from themselves, save them from the inevitable burnout that will occur if other teachers don't step up and take on committee work and other leadership roles within the school, too.

Three-E teachers do not intend to be difficult to work with or obstinate, but sometimes their need for creativity is stronger than their commitment to collaboration. As educators, we're hoping teachers will take the initiative to build on the curriculum models we provide for them, so embrace their creativity. Listen to teachers.

Remember, teachers don't have to be great at everything to model a best practice; they only need to be good at something.

As educators, we're hoping teachers will take the initiative to build on the curriculum models we provide for them, so embrace their creativity. Listen to teachers.

Be flexible! If they see a different path to a district goal and it makes sense, respect their professional judgment and let them try to achieve the goal their way.

Finally, spend time in the classrooms of your best teachers. Excellent teachers are sometimes given little attention in a school because coaches and administrators are so busy with colleagues who are needy. These excellent teachers put so much time and energy into planning and implementing curriculum—and no one ever drops by to say "Great job!" or to see the teacher and students engaged in the good work they do. These teachers don't require lengthy coaching interventions, but stopping by periodically to check out the action, and offer a suggestion or two shows you care and appreciate their commitment to excellence.

It is unlikely that any school will have an entire staff of Three-E teachers. It is a fortunate school indeed that has even a few teachers who fall into this category—a tribute not only to fine coaching, but to good hiring practices. We need to nurture our best teachers to make sure they achieve their potential and remain in the Three-E category.

THE THREE Ts—TRYING HARD, TIMID, TOO STRESSED

Most schools have many teachers who fall into this category. These teachers are "worker bees." They take their responsibilities seriously. They want to do what's best for kids and diligently try to comply with district mandates. They practically memorize the teacher's manual and follow its lead meticulously.

Therein lies the problem. More followers than leaders, they typically lack the confidence to deviate from the familiar and just want to continue to do what they have been doing—possibly for years! Going down a new path is too risky. There is too much to learn, and what if the new curriculum or teaching strategy is less effective than what they are doing right now?

Three-T teachers are easily overloaded. They feel obligated to proceed page by page, ask every comprehension question, and do every follow-up activity. It's a daunting task, given the heft of most curriculum guides.

An even bigger crisis occurs when no teacher's guide is provided. Without the confidence and creativity to strike out on their own, these teachers panic. "But what do we do?" they wail. They go to a workshop on a new literacy practice and come back more frustrated than enlightened. Three-T teachers need to be shown. Sometimes they need to be shown over and over. With enough support, however, they will "get it" and will get on board.

This makes Three-T teachers your most coachable group. These are the teachers who will watch you carefully and, with continued

We need to nurture our best teachers to make sure they achieve their potential and remain in the Three-E category.

Three-T teachers need to be shown. Sometimes they need to be shown over and over. With enough support, however, they will "get it" and will get on board.

coaching, will learn to implement a practice effectively. A full-scale coaching intervention is needed here (not just classroom modeling) with the gradual release of responsibility because Three-T teachers truly believe that you are more capable of good teaching than they are. They will ask you to model lessons endlessly unless you give them a little push: Today I will model. Next time we will co-plan and co-teach. The following day I will come back to watch you try this on your own. (See **Coaching Plan of Action** on page 102 to plan a full coaching intervention for Three-T or other teachers.)

With coaching, most of these teachers will demonstrate a suitable level of competence. The problem is that every innovation will require the same level of implementation energy from you. A few of these Three-T teachers will gain confidence as well as competence somewhere along the way and will discover teaching talents they never knew they had. They will learn to trust their professional instincts and resourcefulness and will evolve into teacher-leaders themselves. For these teachers in particular, you will have performed a wonderful service.

THE THREE Os—ORNERY, OUTSPOKEN, OVERBEARING

Here comes trouble! Teachers in this category can be uncooperative, downright difficult, and highly vocal about their discontent. They regard themselves as superior to you and most of the teachers in the building and are not shy about telling you so—sometimes in a painfully direct manner. Nothing makes them happy, except whatever they are doing in their own little classroom-kingdom. But you have only a general sense of this because they do not share, and they certainly don't invite you into their rooms to find out for yourself.

Three-O teachers can intimidate other teachers, especially their Three-T colleagues. Teachers who might otherwise align themselves with you are afraid to stand up to a grade-level partner who, for instance, argues loudly against a new spelling initiative or writing curriculum.

A problem that coaches and administrators face in dealing with Three-O teachers is that they tend to achieve at least moderate results with their students. They have typically been teaching for a long while and have a solid enough performance history behind them to defend their practices, even when they seem outdated.

You will probably never turn these teachers into your staunchest allies, although you may succeed in changing their practices if the stakes are high enough. Pick your battles! Sometimes instruction that has been "good enough" for the past two decades no longer makes the grade as literacy standards become more stringent.

> Sometimes instruction that has been "good enough" for the past two decades no longer makes the grade as literacy standards become more stringent.

For example, if every teacher in your building is now required to meet with students in small guided-reading groups, it is not okay for Ms. O. to continue to teach whole-class novels to every student in the class every day of the year. That would be a "hill worth dying on," but might also require the intervention of an administrator. You can recommend; the principal can require.

Occasionally Three-O teachers are professionals who at one time fit the Three-E description but, over the course of their career, have allowed their positive energy to turn negative. Somewhere along the way they became disenfranchised. Perhaps they were enthusiastic, forward-thinking teachers early-on, but no one listened. They retreated into their own little classroom world and built walls around themselves rather than bridges to the larger professional community.

Find something to celebrate in the instruction of an ornery Three-O teacher; think of a way to make that practice public, and you may have taken a small step in turning this teacher around. Ask for help: "I love the way you get your students to engage so fully in book discussions. How do you do that? Could you share one or two techniques at our next staff meeting?"

Initially, don't devote too much time to worrying about how to get into Three-O teachers' classrooms to change instruction. Before they can be coached, they need to open their minds to the possibility of change. If you can achieve that, you have served these teachers well.

THE THREE Ds—DULL, DEFEATED, DONE

While Three-O teachers are often too aggressive and outspoken, you at least know where you stand with them. By contrast, teachers in the Three-D category are too passive. They may nod their head in all the right places, but that's about all of the energy they can muster. Regardless of how much you work with them, they barely respond.

These teachers tend to have a rosy view of the past that is more perception than reality: "Kids were different then. Now they can't spell, can't write a decent sentence, and you know nowadays, their families don't really care about education…"

There is little rigor in the classrooms of Three-D teachers, and their expectations are low for themselves and their students. Their classrooms are dull, lifeless places with little on the walls to spark students' interest. Fill-in-the-blank assignments dominate as the teacher instructs from the chair behind his desk.

You feel compelled to do something to serve the needs of Three-D teachers—if not to change their practice in a profound way, at least to rescue the children—who appear to be withering before your eyes. It's not easy. Some of these teachers are willing to go through the motions of implementing a new initiative, if only to stay off the radar

Find something to celebrate in the instruction of an ornery Three-O teacher; think of a way to make that practice public, and you may have taken a small step in turning this teacher around.

of the administrator; they don't want to draw attention to themselves. Others tell you straight out: "I am retiring at the end of the year and I am not going to [make whatever change you are proposing]."

Three-D teachers tend to be near the end of their career. Although many veteran teachers remain committed to cutting-edge practices until the day they walk out of their classroom for the last time, this is not the case for teachers in this category. They are DONE, both mentally and emotionally. So what is a coach to do?

A full-flung coaching initiative with Three-D teachers is probably not the best use of your time. While I generally don't advocate stand-alone lesson-modeling sessions, this may be the most realistic course of action with these teachers. If they watch you teach something—and it looks very, very easy—maybe they will try it that way themselves. And even if they don't make the suggested change, at least you have served the students in the class well by enriching their day with a high-quality literacy lesson.

Reflecting on the Interpersonal Dynamics of Coaching

Navigating interpersonal relationships as a literacy coach is a bit like hugging an amoeba. Regardless of the coaching characteristics you bring to the role, you are at the mercy of people, places, and ever-changing events. From year to year, administrators come and go. There are new curriculum initiatives. New teachers arrive and others leave. A teacher who seemed to fit into the Three-T category last year appears to be moving into the Three-O group this year now that she has changed grade levels and is working with a different team.

Still, thinking about the four categories of teachers described here is useful because now you know what to probably expect from different teacher types. And you have some insights into how you, the literacy coach, can best intervene to serve these teachers.

A next step you can take in thinking about how you will approach teachers with different traits is to fill out the chart included with the study questions at the end of this chapter. When I presented this sheet at a recent workshop, a coach in the audience asked if I wanted her to fill in the boxes with the names of teachers in her building— because she could see where everyone fit.

"NO!" I responded. I definitely do not want coaches to label their teachers. This sheet is to help you identify practices, not people. Think about what you are seeing from teachers within different categories. Then jot down some possible coaching interventions that might be effective with different folks based on the attitudes and dispositions they bring to their classroom each day.

> Regardless of the coaching characteristics you bring to the role, you are at the mercy of people, places, and everchanging events.

STUDY QUESTIONS FOR CHAPTER SIX

1. Think about the coach characteristics described at the beginning of this chapter. Which characteristics are particular strengths that you bring to your role?

2. Is there an area of literacy in which you would like to be more knowledgeable? How could you address this need?

3. Think about the four teacher types described in this chapter. Which teacher type do you personally find the most challenging? How could you change your own attitudes and behaviors in order to make a greater difference with the attitudes and behaviors of these teachers?

Use the following chart to identify behaviors you see from teachers in each category as they are engaged in literacy instruction. How can you provide support?

Teacher Behaviors and Possible Coaching Interventions

WHAT DO YOU SEE? WHAT CAN YOU DO?

Three-E Teachers (Excellent, Energetic, Enthusiastic)	**Three-T Teachers** (Trying hard, Timid, Too stressed)
Three-O Teachers (Ornery, Outspoken, Over-bearing)	**Three-D Teachers** (Defeated, Dull, DONE)

Principles and Protocols of Effective Literacy Coaching

Understanding Principles of Coaching: Frequently Asked Questions

Fitting all of the pieces of coaching together in the day-to-day business of working with teachers seems a daunting task. "What does the coaching process *look* like?" coaches ask me. "Is there a model I can follow to assure that I'm coaching correctly?"

I wish there was one simple formula for "coaching correctly," a process that worked every time. After searching for this one best way over a number of years, I have finally figured out that we are asking the wrong question. The question should not be, "What is the one best coaching model?" The question should be: "What do we need to understand about the coaching process so we can apply the principles of coaching effectively and flexibly day to day?"

If we identify a hard-and-fast model today, all of that might need to change tomorrow because the school gets a new principal, a few teachers leave, there is a different literacy curriculum, or district mandates change. Hitting the mark as a coach is difficult because the target keeps moving.

Following are a few principles that all coaches should consider in order to get started with the coaching process and keep it moving along.

WHO WILL I COACH?

There are three basic options as to who will get coached—teachers who *want* coaching, teachers who *need* coaching, or *all* teachers. The option that is selected and guides the coach's work is often decided *for* coaches rather than *by* them. Some districts view coaching as a component of the long-term professional development for the entire staff. In that case, all teachers will have access to the literacy coach in their building at some point during the school year. For example, the coach may work with the second-grade teachers on fluency this month, and move on to first-grade phonics next month.

The benefit of this all-school approach is that everyone has access to the coach in a systematic manner and professional development is tied closely to the real needs of teachers in a building, not some assumed need identified by district personnel who bring in an "expert" to deliver a generic workshop. The downside of this option is that there is no significant differentiation in the level of support provided by the coach to individual teachers. The strongest teacher of literacy in the school may get the same time and attention and kind of support from the coach as the brand-new teacher who is struggling.

Another view that guides the selection of which teachers will get coached is the stance that coaching can only be effective when the teacher *wants* to be coached. While of course it would be wonderful if we could get all teachers to the point where they were chasing after the coach begging, "Work with me! Work with me!," I doubt that will happen any time soon. If the coach worked solely with teachers eager for coaching, he'd spend most of his time with the Three-E teachers described in the previous chapter. As indicated there, these terrific teachers both need and deserve coaching, but the ones who are most needy are the Three-T teachers who may be too insecure and hesitant to ask for help, and the Three-O and Three-D folks who don't want the help but clearly need it. I think it is unrealistic to think that coaching will ever truly change instruction in a school where the only teachers who get coached are the ones who seek out the coach.

> In order to change student learning, schools need to change the instruction of teachers whose students are not achieving.

In order to change student learning, schools need to change the instruction of teachers whose students are not achieving. This brings us to the third option, the teachers who *need* coaching. Unless there is a *district plan* in place or a specific *philosophy* that guides the coaching process, a coach's time in most schools is spent with the teachers identified as needing assistance to improve student performance. Sometimes a principal will tell a coach, "I want you to work with Ms. W. in third grade," or "Take a peek in Mr. B.'s fifth grade and tell me if you think he's teaching guided reading correctly." Other times the coach approaches the principal: "I think I should spend some time with Ms. G. in kindergarten."

> We should continuously analyze our practice so that how we teach tomorrow is always a little better than how we taught today.

A particularly nasty spin on this view of coaching teachers who *need* support is the perception that this sends a message to the teacher that he or she needs to be "fixed." That is a dangerous and counter-productive means of describing the situation. Instead, we need to communicate to our colleagues that, just as we take students from "where they are" and move them forward with their learning, the same is true for us as educators. We should continuously analyze our practice so that how we teach tomorrow is always a little better than how we taught today.

While there should be a mix of all teacher types on a coach's agenda, the answer to "who gets coached?" will in most cases be the teachers for whom coaching can make the biggest difference in improving student learning.

HOW LONG SHOULD I COACH A PARTICULAR TEACHER?

It depends! Some teachers, like some students, will catch on quickly, while others will require more time. Central to the duration of your focus on a particular teacher will be a clear understanding on the part of both the coach and the teacher that coaching is a *process*. It is not an isolated *event* that occurs once and then is all over. Neither is it repeated modeling by the coach, day after day, until the teacher decides she feels comfortable enough to implement the practice on her own. Remember that the goal of coaching is teacher independence and that the means of getting there should be the gradual release of responsibility—that same explicit model we apply to students' learning.

In the next section of this chapter, where various protocols for the coaching process are described, there is a "Coaching Plan of Action" that is divided into four sessions. In many cases, four sessions will be enough to make a difference in a specified area of literacy instruction. Of course, the plan can be modified to make it shorter or longer.

The length of time a coach stays with one teacher will be determined by other factors as well. One of these variables will be the classroom teacher's follow-through. There are some teachers who resist change because the old way was easier or seemed less risky, or they simply don't want the coach intruding on their professional decision making. In other words, some teachers are capable of making the necessary instructional changes but choose not to do so.

Now, as a coach, you are faced with a dilemma: If you walk away from this teacher, you are sending the message that all it takes is enough resistance and you (the coach) will quietly ride off into the sunset. On the other hand, how long are you going to hang in there with a teacher who is keeping you from working with other teachers who may be more eager for your assistance and who *will* implement important instructional changes?

This is a place where an administrator may provide the needed impetus for change: The teacher *will* provide small-group instruction to the lowest-performing students every single day. The coach and the principal can both monitor the requested instructional modification— and the coach can move on to a different teacher more tuned in to the coaching process.

Remember that the goal of coaching is teacher independence and that the means of getting there should be the gradual release of responsibility— that same explicit model we apply to students' learning.

HOW MANY TEACHERS SHOULD I COACH AT ONCE?

How much time do you have available for coaching? Think of this in terms of the number of hours you have available for coaching daily. Do you have one hour? Then one teacher is probably all you can manage. Two hours? That might be enough for two teachers, unless you need to be with a particular teacher for the entire literacy block. Even if you have three or more hours available for coaching, I would generally not advocate working with more than two teachers at a time.

Most coaches serve multiple roles within their building, including providing direct services to students—a task we never want to give up entirely for reasons discussed in **Chapter Six**. That will limit the time most school literacy leaders can devote to coaching. In my experience, however, you need to push yourself beyond working with just one teacher at a time because, in most buildings, there are many teachers who need coaching. Your progress will be too slow if you don't work with two teachers simultaneously. The trick is to bring teachers into the process at different times so that while your work with one is intense, your work with another is less strenuous. Maybe you are observing and modeling in your second classroom. In your first classroom, you have progressed to the point where you are returning to watch the teacher's independent application of a practice you have coached.

> The trick is to bring teachers into the process at different times so that while your work with one is intense, your work with another is less strenuous.

HOW DO I GET STARTED WITH COACHING?

If you are new to coaching, or if coaching is new to your school, consider beginning with a teacher with whom you anticipate fairly quick success. You will be tempted to take on the most challenging teacher in order to make a significant difference to student learning, but resist that urge. You may actually want to begin with a Three-E teacher who needs just a little support to set the tone that coaching is for everyone! Your initial coaching may then produce a model classroom where you can bring other teachers to see good literacy instruction in action.

Another consideration in choosing a place to begin is the classroom-management strategies the teacher has in place. You really can't work on literacy until the teacher has basic classroom routines in hand. I have confronted poor classroom management many times and it is a no-win situation: The teacher appears eager for your coaching expertise, but when you arrive, you find that what she really wants is for you to deal with (in the space of an hour) all of the behavior problems that have been escalating since the beginning of the school year. Addressing these issues is not the job of the literacy coach. You can help the teacher get help. But your time and talents are better spent with a teacher whose classroom climate and management allow the nurturing of instructional skills.

Regardless of the way you select the teacher you will coach, at some point, you will have to take that first critical step in initiating the coaching process. What will you say in order to set a positive tone? Sometimes the focus of the coaching will have been predetermined by a district mandate or an administrative "suggestion." Your task in this case is to find a gentle, non-threatening way of communicating this to the teacher: "As you know, this year all of the second grades will be implementing a new fluency program. The principal has asked that I spend part of my time supporting you as you get started with this."

Perhaps you have the luxury of beginning where the teacher would like to start. Although there are many ways you can approach teachers, there are a few questions that lead to a dead end: Avoid questions like, "What can I do to help you?" First, this implies that you are the expert and the teacher is less than competent. Furthermore, if the teacher answers, "Nothing," that's pretty much the end of the conversation.

The question, in my experience, which leads to the best conversation is, "What is it about teaching literacy that keeps you awake at night?" I think this question works because teachers don't see it as a coaching question; they see it as an interesting question! Everyone has something they worry about in the teaching of reading and writing, and this question begins to get those worries out in the open.

A teacher might say, "I worry about getting everything done I need to accomplish within my ninety-minute literacy block." Or she might say, "I've never had kids this low in fourth grade, kids who have no idea how to write a complete sentence."

Acknowledge the teacher's frustration: "Now that we have that new intervention program, our morning schedule is even more packed than it was last year." Or, "I know you have a group of really low fourth graders this year; I saw the scores." Then you can offer to work on the problem together. Of course, this doesn't assure total teacher compliance, but you have at least made a good start.

HOW DO I TALK WITH THE TEACHER ABOUT INSTRUCTION THAT NEEDS TO BE CHANGED?

There are a few guidelines we hear over and over about techniques for coaches to communicate with teachers: Listen 80% of the time; talk 20% of the time. Let the teacher take the lead in telling *you* what she regarded as the strengths and weaknesses of her instruction. Build on the teacher's strengths.

No one would dispute the wisdom of any of these principles. However, there comes a time when you will ask the teacher, "How do you think it went?" and she will say "Great!" (The lesson was far from "great.") You will listen endlessly and eventually wish there was an "off"

The question, in my experience, which leads to the best conversation is, "What is it about teaching literacy that keeps you awake at night?"

Let the teacher take the lead in telling you what she regarded as the strengths and weaknesses of her instruction. Build on the teacher's strengths.

button. What the teacher asks for has little to do with the roadblocks that really stood in the way of her teaching success—and it's a stretch to find even one legitimate "strength" to launch the work you will do together.

In other words, you have to say the hard stuff. To make it even more awkward, this is the same lady you sit next to at lunch nearly every day and now you have to find a way to tell her that her small-group instruction is substandard. Of course, you won't say it *that* way. But how *will* you say it? Sometimes I rehearse my words in my mind until I think I can convey my message in a voice that is simultaneously humble, caring, competent, and clear.

Giving yourself some space between the classroom visit and the follow-up debriefing will allow you to find the right tone and language to say what you must say. While it is never a good idea for the coach to "score" the teacher on her instruction, taking some notes on what was observed will ground the dialogue in evidence rather than interpretation. The protocols described in the next part of this chapter provide a framework for coaching conversations that are logically sequenced and lead to analysis and action rather than emotional responses and hurt feelings.

I keep a clipboard handy with a stack of different protocols. As I move from classroom to classroom, I retrieve the form best suited to that particular coaching need and use it to document my work. By the end of the day I have two or three protocols filled out that I then move to a binder for safekeeping and future reference.

Understanding the Coaching Protocols

In the final part of this chapter, I present fourteen coaching protocols and a description of how each may be used by literacy coaches as they support teachers. Using these protocols or others you create to meet your coaching needs will help you establish *your* coaching model—at least for this year. Next year you may need to use the protocols differently. Your coaching process should be unique to you and the teachers you serve. It will evolve in response to the shared vision of everyone in your learning community, your knowledge of best literacy practices, and your skills as a coach. Email coachingprotocols@maupinhouse.com for Word documents of the protocols so you can expand and modify them according to your specific needs.

THE COACHING PROTOCOLS

Planning for Coaching
• Literacy Needs Assessment
• Coaching Plan of Action

Analyzing Literacy Instruction
• Checklist for Setting the Stage for Literacy Learning
• Checklist for Building Literacy Knowledge
• Checklist for Reinforcing Literacy Knowledge

Monitoring and Reflecting on the Classroom Environment and Management
• Classroom Environment Checklist
• Classroom Management Checklist

Monitoring and Reflecting on Literacy Instruction
• Protocol for Monitoring Instruction That Gradually Releases Responsibility to Students
• Protocol for Coach's Observation and Conferring
• Protocol for Reflecting on Small-Group Instruction and Independent Activities
• Protocol for Reflecting on a Model Lesson
• Protocol for Teacher Self-Reflection

Incorporating Administrators' Support
• Protocol for Reflecting on Coaching
• Administrator's Monitoring Protocol

Planning for Coaching

• Literacy Needs Assessment
• Coaching Plan of Action

Coaching that makes a difference is both intentional and systematic. The two protocols described below, **Literacy Needs Assessment** and **Coaching Plan of Action**, are tools coaches can use to first define an area of need and then set up a step-by-step means of addressing that need, one teacher at a time.

LITERACY NEEDS ASSESSMENT

The **Literacy Needs Assessment** is a good document for coaches to use as they take their first step in planning for systematic change. Use the form provided here, or design one that addresses the specific areas of need for your building. Ask teachers to prioritize their top three needs. Then analyze the feedback you receive for individual teachers, grade levels, or even your whole faculty. Do patterns emerge or does everyone seem to need something different? Take this information into account as you set your coaching agenda.

Such autonomy may not always be possible. But when it is, listen to what your teachers are telling you. Honoring their voice shows that coaching is about *their* needs—and that's the message you want to convey.

COACHING PLAN OF ACTION

The **Coaching Plan of Action** forms the skeleton of the coach's and classroom teacher's agenda as they plan their work together over the long haul and provides opportunities for incorporating other forms and protocols included in this chapter. Developing this plan collaboratively will make it clear that both partners need to be invested in the coaching process. The first decision that the coach and teacher will need to make together is: What is our goal?

Note that this plan calls for a four-session coaching sequence. The first session is not devoted to modeling as many teachers would prefer. They plead, "Come into my classroom and show me how to..." Good coaches realize that they will do a better job of supporting the teacher if they have a more solid understanding of where the teacher is presently succeeding or failing with the identified instructional practice. The first session therefore begins with a lesson where the teacher teaches and the coach watches. Fill in the boxes on the **Coaching Plan of Action** as you progress through the four-session sequence.

For the first visit, record the date and focus of the visit: What will the teacher teach? Ask the teacher what resources will be used to teach the lesson, and talk with her about the protocol you would like to bring with you to document your observations. (Two possibilities would be the **Protocol for Monitoring Instruction That Gradually Releases Responsibility to Students** or the **Protocol for Coach's Observation and Conferring,** both described later in this chapter.) Offer to give the teacher a copy of your notes after the visit and explain how you would like to use what you have written as the basis for a follow-up conversation. If you would like to include an administrator in the lesson debriefing, this is a good time to talk about that as well. You can also explain that the final column on the form, "Follow-up professional conversation to prepare for next visit," will be filled in at the time of the debriefing to identify additional literacy content knowledge that might be helpful to the teacher and which you (the coach) may be able to provide before the next classroom visit.

Plan to model a lesson for the teacher during the second visit in the coaching sequence. This time it is the coach who will identify the resources that will be used. Suggest that the teacher fill in the **Protocol for Reflecting on a Model Lesson** as she watches you present your lesson. Is there something else you could share with the teacher

The first decision that the coach and teacher will need to make together is: What is our goal?

related to literacy content? Add that to the "professional conversation" box in the second row.

For the third visit, the coach and teacher should plan the lesson together. This allows the teacher to implement some of the instructional strategies modeled during the coach's demonstration lesson. It also allows the coach to clarify any points about which the teacher is confused. The coach and teacher can co-teach the lesson, too. Try to get the teacher to take the instructional lead and offer support only when necessary. However, some teachers will still be insecure about flying solo and will want the coach to participate more actively. A useful protocol to document this phase of the coaching process might be the **Protocol for Teacher Self-Reflection**. But rather than asking the teacher to write out responses to each question, the teacher might prefer to respond orally, using this protocol to guide the conversation. The coach can take a few notes if desired.

Some teachers will need a more gradual transition to independence, but ideally, by the fourth visit, the teacher should be ready to plan and teach a lesson alone related to the coaching goal. That doesn't mean the instruction will be perfect or that the coaching is "finished," but there needs to be some accountability for your time—and the teacher's. This fourth session is a good point at which to take stock of how far you've come and where you and the teacher need to go from here.

The role of the coach now is essentially what it was during the first visit: to observe. Documenting this observation with the same form used initially, **Protocol for Monitoring Instruction That Gradually Releases Responsibility to Students** or the **Protocol for Coach's Observation and Conferring**, will allow the coach and teacher to measure the progress that has taken place over the four classroom visits.

Note that other "actions" are specified at the bottom of the **Coaching Plan of Action**.

> **Looking at student work.** Are there student work samples that the coach and teacher could examine together as evidence of improved teaching practices? Remember that the real test of a coach's success is not just improved teaching, but improved student learning. What kind of student work will attest to the value of the instruction you have worked so hard to promote? A coaching plan should always include some kind of student evidence, as in the end, this is what counts. If the teaching looks terrific, but the learning hasn't moved forward, no one will get too excited about the value of coaching.

> **Professional reading.** Is there a journal article or a book that could support this teacher as she learns more about this area of literacy?

Try to get the teacher to take the instructional lead and offer support only when necessary.

Teachers count on their coaches to know a lot about literacy. Good coaches make a point of staying current in their knowledge of professional literature—the findings of recent research or theory translated into classroom practice—and knowledgeable analyses of what works and what doesn't in different teaching situations.

Classroom visits. Are there other classrooms in the school or district where the teacher could see the identified instructional practice in action? Classroom teachers don't get out much! They are, for the most part, confined to their own classroom and have limited knowledge of what is happening in other parts of their district—or even other rooms in their own school. Coaches, on the other hand, have the opportunity to check out the action in many classrooms. By talking to their coach colleagues they also acquire a sense of where good things are happening elsewhere in the district. Coaches should take advantage of this broad view to connect their teachers with other teachers and classrooms where they can see best practices modeled.

Family/community involvement. Is there a way to enlist the support of families or the larger community to help the teacher achieve the goal she has established? In too many schools, parents are an untapped resource. While there are certainly parents who are not available during the day to support the work of the classroom, there are other parents or caregivers with both the time and interest to lend a hand. Sometimes teachers are unsure of how to rally parent support—and what to do with the parents once they arrive. Coaches can help: Are there classrooms where parents could support children practicing their reading fluency? Could they provide daily sight-word review in a primary grade? How about reading aloud to a child or two? Coaches can coordinate an initiative that incorporates parents and community members into the day-to-day fabric of schoolwide literacy.

Considering these additional actions will help the coach and teacher plan meaningfully for the coaching experience. Both protocols for planning for coaching, the **Literacy Needs Assessment** and **Coaching Plan of Action** are presented on the following pages.

LITERACY NEEDS ASSESSMENT

Name: _____   Grade: _____   Date: _____

Please number in order of importance (1-5) the areas in which you would like additional support to teach reading and writing more effectively (1 = most urgent area of need).

_____ Establishing a literacy-rich classroom environment

_____ Grouping students appropriately for small-group instruction and matching instruction to students' skill needs

_____ Selecting texts for use during shared, guided, and independent reading

_____ Planning for comprehensive literacy instruction

_____ Incorporating state test objectives meaningfully into literacy instruction

_____ Supporting students before reading

_____ Teaching the metacognitive comprehension strategies (connecting, picturing, wondering, predicting, noticing, figuring out) for use <u>during</u> reading

_____ Engaging students in high-level conversations about text

_____ Teaching students to respond in writing to open-ended comprehension questions

_____ Differentiating instruction during independent-work time (the workshop component) of the literacy block

_____ Helping students to become reflective readers and writers

_____ Developing rubrics for different literacy tasks and using them to collect and chart data

_____ Teaching phonological awareness and word-study skills at my grade level

_____ Improving students' reading fluency

_____ Teaching vocabulary meaningfully

_____ Teaching language conventions meaningfully (spelling, grammar, usage)

_____ Developing students' oral language skills

_____ Teaching narrative/expository/persuasive writing for CMT (and other) purposes

_____ Teaching the writing traits and author's craft (beyond the CMT)

_____ Integrating reading and writing with content-area instruction

_____ Creating author studies and genre studies

COACHING PLAN OF ACTION

Teacher: _____   Coach: _____   Date: _____

Goal: _____

Action	Date	Focus of visit and materials used	Protocols used	Follow-up professional conversation to prepare for next visit
First visit: baseline data				
Second visit: model				
Third visit: co-plan/co-teach				
Fourth visit: teacher independence				
Other actions: • Looking at student work: • Professional reading: • Classroom visits: • Family/community involvement: • Other:				

Analyzing Literacy Instruction

- Checklist for Setting the Stage for Literacy Learning
- Checklist for Building Literacy Knowledge
- Checklist for Reinforcing Literacy Knowledge

I think it would be a bit cumbersome to bring three checklists into a classroom when analyzing literacy instruction. It might also raise a teacher's suspicions about whether coaching was more about support or more about evaluation if he saw you arrive with a multi-page document with little boxes to check off. Instead, these checklists can be used effectively with classroom teachers before you ever step foot into a classroom. Classroom teachers should know what we are looking for in explicit literacy instruction, and these checklists are a perfect place to begin in raising their level of awareness. Introduce one checklist at a time at a faculty or grade-level meeting. Give teachers time to digest the information and ask questions.

These checklists can also be used after a coach has begun work in a classroom as the coach and teacher analyze together whether particular components of instruction were present or absent in a lesson taught by the teacher or modeled by the coach. These checklists provide a powerful lens through which to view the fine points of literacy teaching.

Review **Chapters Two**, **Three**, and **Four** for a close-up examination of what explicit literacy instruction should look like as teachers set the stage, build knowledge, and reinforce knowledge—as well as what we see in classrooms when explicit literacy instruction has gone off track.

CHECKLIST FOR SETTING THE STAGE FOR LITERACY LEARNING

Teacher: _____   Date: _____

Administrator's key: **0**=Not present   **1**=Somewhat present   **2**=Competent   **3**=Exemplary

Look For	Score	Comment
GETTING STUDENTS TO CARE		
1. Teacher lets students know how this work will help to make them more successful now.		
2. Teacher conveys to students that they *will* be successful.		
3. Teacher clarifies routines and waits until students are focused before moving on with the lesson.		
4. Teacher encourages positive body language.		
5. Teacher demonstrates enthusiasm for the topic and sets a positive tone.		
6. Teacher uses concrete object or graphic to get students' attention when appropriate.		
ACTIVATING/BUILDING PRIOR KNOWLEDGE		
1. Teacher links new knowledge to what students already know about the topic, author, genre, skill, or strategy.		
2. Teacher asks for just a few connections from students before moving on and sticks to the time frame.		
3. Teacher monitors students' background knowledge; modifies objective accordingly.		
4. Teacher activates background knowledge that is relevant.		
5. Teacher introduces vocabulary that supports the lesson.		
IDENTIFYING OBJECTIVES		
1. Teacher has one (and only one) clearly defined objective.		
2. Teacher selects an objective that is both important and rigorous.		
3. Teacher selects an objective that is measurable and achievable within the scope of the lesson.		
4. Teacher communicates objective to students. (Both oral and written communication is best.)		
5. Teacher clarifies for students their accountability in meeting the objective.		

Areas of greatest strength: _____

_____

Next steps in enhancing teaching in Phase I of explicit instruction: _____

_____

CHECKLIST FOR BUILDING LITERACY KNOWLEDGE

Teacher: _____   Date: _____

Administrator's key: **0**=Not present **1**= Somewhat present **2**=Competent   **3**=Exemplary

Look For	Score	Comment
EXPLAINING		
1. The explanation includes hints or steps to clarify the process needed to succeed at the task.		
2. The explanation is brief, focused, clear, and stated in grade-appropriate language.		
3. The explanation actively engages students.		
MODELING		
1. The teacher has planned carefully for the modeling portion of the lesson.		
2. If a text is used for modeling, it is a good match for the lesson's objective.		
3. The teacher's modeling demonstrates solid understanding of the skill/strategy/concept.		
4. The teacher links the modeling to the explanation that preceded it so students will understand the process.		
5. The teacher models her thinking in the present tense, not as thinking she did in the past.		
6. The teacher monitors students' understanding during modeling in order to know when to move on to bridging.		
BRIDGING		
1. Bridging (structured student practice) extends for a substantial length of time—7-10 minutes.		
2. The teacher prompts students where necessary to help them succeed.		
3. The teacher provides many repetitions to build students' confidence and competence.		
4. The teacher monitors students' performance in order to identify appropriate follow-up scaffolding.		
5. The teacher facilitates a smooth transition to the next phase of instruction whereby students know what to do and how their learning will be measured.		

Areas of greatest strength: _____

_____

Next steps in enhancing teaching in Phase II of explicit instruction: _____

_____

CHECKLIST FOR REINFORCING LITERACY KNOWLEDGE

Teacher: _____   Date: _____

Administrator's key: **0**=Not present   **1**=Somewhat present   **2**=Competent   **3**=Exemplary

Look For	Score	Comment
GUIDED PRACTICE		
1. The teacher works with students in small groups using texts at students' instructional level.		
2. The small-group lesson has a clear objective and adheres to a "gradual release" instructional model with most of the group time devoted to practice.		
3. There is a high level of engagement and discussion during small-group instruction focused on students' active construction of meaning.		
4. The teacher "troubleshoots" by conferring briefly as s/he circulates among students.		
INDEPENDENT PRACTICE		
1. An appropriate amount of time is devoted to independent reading of "just-right books" (between 5 an 20 minutes depending on the grade.)		
2. There is some form of student accountability to a learning objective for independent reading.		
3. Authentic activities supporting learning objectives are provided within multiple dimensions of the literacy curriculum: phonemic awareness, phonics, fluency, vocabulary, comprehension, writing, and oral language.		
4. Activities to reinforce learning are differentiated according to students' literacy needs and performance level.		
5. The teacher demonstrates good management of independent activities along with the implementation of guided practice.		
REFLECTION		
1. The teacher asks students to talk about what they learned today as readers and writers and how they think this will connect to tomorrow's literacy work.		
2. The teacher asks students to share evidence from their independent reading or application activities that demonstrates mastery of the objective.		

Areas of greatest strength: _____

_____

Next steps in enhancing teaching in Phase III of explicit instruction: _____

_____

Monitoring and Reflecting on the Classroom Environment and Classroom Management

Literacy learning does not occur in a vacuum. It takes place in the context of a learning community that either enhances or inhibits its progress. That is why both the classroom environment and classroom management are so critical to the well-being of children as readers and writers. The following protocols will help coaches and teachers analyze these dimensions of the literacy context more deeply.

CLASSROOM ENVIRONMENT CHECKLIST

The **Classroom Environment Checklist** is a good form to use whether you are simply assessing features of the literacy environment or you are analyzing literacy instruction more comprehensively. Examining the way classroom space and materials are organized, what is on the walls, and what is celebrated in the classroom will provide a fairly reliable predictor of the kind of instruction that occurs there. After talking with teachers about *what* is important to a positive classroom environment and *why* these components contribute to a positive literacy experience for students, teachers can be given the form to reflect on their own classroom environment, noting both its strengths and the areas that still need some work.

CLASSROOM MANAGEMENT CHECKLIST

As noted in **Chapter One**, general features of classroom management are not really the domain of the literacy coach. Still, these factors could be the reason that literacy instruction is not moving forward in a classroom. At the very least, the literacy coach might want to alert the classroom teacher to essential elements of classroom management that need to be addressed and help to connect a classroom teacher with issues in this area to an administrator or other support staff who can provide the necessary assistance. The **Classroom Management Checklist** offers a starting point for thinking about the specifics of management problems that often get in the way of student learning.

CLASSROOM ENVIRONMENT CHECKLIST

Teacher: _____   Date: _____

Administrator's key: **0**=Not present **1**=Somewhat present **2**=Competent **3**=Exemplary

Look For	Score	Comment
1. Current work is displayed that demonstrates the power of students' thinking.		
2. Displayed work includes the lesson objective.		
3. Displayed work includes feedback to students that is specific and matched to published criteria for assessing that type of task.		
4. Rubrics or criteria charts are accessible to students and presented in a manner that is meaningful to children at this grade level.		
5. Data is displayed in a positive manner that enhances students' motivation to set and meet high academic standards.		
6. The room is inviting and lively, but does not appear cluttered or contain "visual overload."		
7. Appropriate word walls are present and students use them.		
8. There is a sufficient number of books in the classroom of different genres and different reading levels, both fiction and nonfiction.		
9. Books are easily accessible to students, organized in a meaningful way, and attractively displayed.		
10. The classroom is "print rich" with grade-level-appropriate resources, labels, etc.		
11. There is evidence that technology is integrated into students' daily literacy experiences.		
12. There are clearly defined areas for whole class work, small-group work, and individual activities.		
13. The room arrangement supports collaboration and conversation and allows for easy access to students who need assistance.		
14. Any literacy centers present in the classroom show evidence of authentic tasks matched to specific objectives rather than generic activities with no obvious purpose linked to students' defined needs.		
15. The classroom environment conveys a sense of community that is welcoming and low risk.		
16. There is a sense that important things are happening in this classroom, that the curriculum is rigorous and promotes higher levels of thinking.		

Areas of greatest strength: _____

_____

Next steps in enhancing the classroom environment: _____

_____

CLASSROM MANAGEMENT CHECKLIST

Teacher: _____   **Date:** _____

Administrator's key: 0=Not present   **1** =Somewhat present   **2**=Competent   **3**=Exemplary

Look For	Score	Comment
1. **Establishes clear routines for classroom procedures**, especially procedures for working independently while the teacher is engaged in small-group instruction		
2. **Establishes clear expectations for student behavior** that promote mutual respect among teacher and students		
3. **Paces and orchestrates instruction** so that there is no downtime; the teaching is intense		
4. **Holds students to high, rigorous expectations** through the depth and breadth of the curriculum		
5. **Spends more time on academics than non-academics** within all phases of comprehensive literacy		
6. **Intentionally raises the level of classroom talk** with a focus on oral language development within academic discussions		
7. **Organizes materials** for easy access and retrieval.		
8. **Creates emotional climate that is positive and low risk** so that students feel validated and supported		
9. **Transitions** students smoothly from one activity and place to another		
10. **Other:**		

Areas of greatest strength: _____

_____

Next steps in enhancing classroom management: _____

_____

_____

Monitoring and Reflecting on Literacy Instruction

- Protocol for Monitoring Instruction That Gradually Releases Responsibility to Students
- Protocol for Coach's Observation and Conferring
- Protocol for Reflecting on Small-Group Instruction and Independent Activities
- Protocol for Reflecting on a Model Lesson
- Protocol for Teacher Self-Reflection

Coaches need a reliable way of documenting what they see happening during classroom literacy instruction. Such documentation can be largely a matter of personal preference based on a coach's level of familiarity with components of explicit teaching and the way a coach is most comfortable recording his observations. Any protocol used should meet two criteria: 1) It should highlight what was observed, not an interpretation of what was observed, and 2) it should provide a launching point for the follow-up lesson debriefing. The **Protocol for Monitoring Instruction That Gradually Releases Responsibility to Students, Protocol for Coach's Observation and Conferring**, and **Protocol for Reflecting on Small-Group Instruction and Independent Activities** serve my needs as I observe teachers in action. If they don't feel "just right" for you as you coach, of course they can be modified.

Likewise, classroom teachers also need a framework for documenting their observations and reflections as they observe lessons modeled by the coach and reflect on their own instructional practices. The **Protocol for Reflecting on a Model Lesson** and the **Protocol for Teacher Self-Reflection** are designed to meet these needs.

PROTOCOL FOR MONITORING INSTRUCTION THAT GRADUALLY RELEASES RESPONSIBILITY TO STUDENTS

This protocol is a good one for coaches and administrators to use who are somewhat familiar with the model of explicit instruction but still need the framework to alert them to all of the essential components and the instructional sequence. When I use this form, I jot down notes about what I see (the evidence), not my evaluation of what is taking place. Once teachers have been introduced to this instructional model, this protocol is helpful in a follow-up conference with the teacher to reflect together on where the teaching was strong and where it went off track. The spaces at the bottom of the page are useful for noting factors beyond the lesson itself in the areas of classroom environment and general classroom management that may be impacting literacy learning.

PROTOCOL FOR COACH'S OBSERVATION AND CONFERRING

This is the protocol I use the most because it accomplishes so many goals in a brief space. It is most useful, however, to coaches or administrators who know the explicit instructional model so well that they no longer need the framework in the monitoring form described previously in order to quickly and accurately identify the components present in a teacher's instruction. When I am watching a lesson, I make notes about what I am seeing in the "Observations" column, and if it is something to which I want to be sure to respond later, I draw an arrow to the "Comments/Questions/Suggestions" column and make a note there about the point I wish to address. This middle column becomes the focus of the follow-up conference which includes the teacher, the coach, and, when possible, the principal.

Having all of the stakeholders at the table together is the key to coaching success. As we talk about the strengths of the lesson, and how the teacher can build on these strengths to improve her practice, everyone at that table will play a role. The third column, "Expectations for Follow-up," specifies this accountability: What will the teacher do? How will the coach support the teacher? How will the administrator support the teacher? The date of the next visit is identified and recorded on the bottom of the page, thereby establishing a timeline for these follow-up actions. "The next step" clarifies how the coaching process will move forward during the subsequent classroom visit.

PROTOCOL FOR REFLECTING ON SMALL-GROUP INSTRUCTION AND INDEPENDENT ACTIVITIES

A major focus of my work recently, and an initiative in nearly every school I visit, is to get teachers to implement small-group instruction more consistently. This is particularly apparent at the intermediate grade level. Most primary classrooms have small-group instruction in place, though the teaching could benefit from a more explicit focus (one specific objective rather than simply practicing a loosely defined set of word-level strategies). More troublesome is that many intermediate-grade classrooms (grades three and above) don't even have a structure in place for incorporating small-group instruction into daily literacy instruction.

The major dilemma with small-group instruction is that its success is contingent upon so much more than the teaching that happens in the small group. Additionally, you need to look at the classroom environment and classroom management and the productivity of the concurrent independent activities in which students are engaged. The **Protocol for Reflecting on Small-Group Instruction and Independent Activities** offers a means of reflecting deeply on this phase of instruction identified earlier as "reinforcing learning."

Having all of the stakeholders at the table together is the key to coaching success. As we talk about the strengths of the lesson, and how the teacher can build on these strengths to improve her practice, everyone at that table will play a role.

PROTOCOL FOR REFLECTING ON A MODEL LESSON

When teachers watch a model lesson, whether it is delivered by the coach or a teaching colleague, they need a way to focus their thinking. Providing a form to record their observations is a good place to begin. The **Protocol for Reflecting on a Model Lesson** encourages teachers to think about not only *what* they are seeing, but *why* the lesson is effective (or not effective)—with the lesson's objective as the main point of reference. The data collected by teachers becomes a springboard to the follow-up discussion with the teacher (or coach) who modeled the lesson, the observing teacher(s), and the coach. Note that inviting a few teachers to observe the same model lesson is both efficient and effective in generating professional dialogue about the components of good instruction. Remember that no observation is complete until a visiting teacher has reached a conclusion about something he saw that he would now like to try in his own classroom.

PROTOCOL FOR TEACHER SELF-REFLECTION

A colleague once quipped to me that if we could get teachers to do more reflecting on their own instruction, lots of coaches might be out of a job. While that is probably overly optimistic, it is certainly true that many of the insights gained through teacher-coach collaboration could be achieved by teachers themselves if they were a little more analytical about their practices. The **Protocol for Teacher Self-Reflection** gives teachers a step-by-step framework for asking those tough questions that may lead to some professional "ah-ha" moments. It is one thing to *think* a lesson went well; it's sometimes more challenging to point to the evidence that *shows* that the lesson was a success. This form pushes teachers past the easy question—"What did you do?"—to a deeper understanding of *why* the lesson worked or didn't work, how they might revise the lesson for greater impact the next time around, and how they will build on today's outcomes to plan and implement tomorrow's instruction. While teachers may *write* their responses to the questions on this form, *writing* their "answers" is not as important as thinking and talking honestly about their perceptions. Teachers can do that alone or with the support of their coach.

PROTOCOL FOR MONITORING INSTRUCTION
THAT GRADUALLY RELEASES RESPONSIBILITY TO STUDENTS

Teacher: _____   **Administrator/Coach:** _____

Date: _____   **Class/Grade:** _____

Setting the stage for learning	Notes
Getting students to care	
Activating/building prior knowledge	
Identifying objectives	

Building new knowledge	Notes
Explaining	
Modeling	
Bridging	

Reinforcing knowledge	Notes
Guided practice	
Independent practice	
Reflection	

Noteworthy features of classroom environment and classroom management:

_____

_____

_____

PROTOCOL FOR COACH'S OBSERVATION AND CONFERRING

Teacher: _____   Coach: _____   Date: _____

Focus of visit: _____

Observations	Comments/Questions/Suggestions	Expectations for Follow-up
		Teacher:
		Coach:
		Administrator:

Next Visit

Date: _____

Focus of visit:

PROTOCOL FOR REFLECTING ON SMALL-GROUP INSTRUCTION AND INDEPENDENT ACTIVITIES

Teacher: _____   Administrator/Coach: _____

Date: _____   Class/Grade: _____

Criteria	Comments or ✓
Classroom environment	
The arrangement of desks facilitates collaboration when appropriate.	
There is an area designated for small-group instruction.	
There is space for students to work independently.	
There is a classroom library with books accessible to students for independent reading.	
There is a chart prominently displayed in the classroom to help students choose "just-right" books according to their level and interest.	
Reading strategy posters are displayed for students' easy reference.	
Classroom management	
There are management routines in place that facilitate efficient teaching and learning during small-group instruction/independent activities—and students abide by these standards.	
Transitions are smooth with minimal down time.	
The teaching moves at a pace that keeps everyone's attention.	
Positive reinforcement prevails as a means of keeping students on-track.	
Small-group instruction	
Small-group instruction with concurrent independent activities follows shared reading for 60 minutes or more each day.	
The teacher works with 3-4 small groups every day during the literacy blocks, with each group comprised of 3-8 students.	
The small-group lesson is focused on one specific objective matched to the needs of students in that group; the teacher identifies the objective for students.	
There is a weekly group rotation identified by the teacher that specifies which groups will meet each day, and the focus area that will be addressed (comprehension, fluency, word work, vocabulary, etc.).	
Each group meets for approximately 15-20 minutes.	
There is evidence that the teacher has planned for the small-group lesson. This includes familiarity with the text, knowledgeable modeling, organization, and accessibility of materials.	
There is evidence of scaffolding (gradually releasing responsibility) to help students become more independent in meeting the lesson objective: modeling and practice.	
High-level discussion about text is a central feature of the small-group work, with much student interaction and engagement. (The students talk more than the teacher.)	
The teacher uses techniques other than "round robin" reading to check students' oral reading fluency.	
Independent activities	
Daily independent activities always include independent reading with some form of accountability (journal response, use of sticky notes, etc.).	
There is evidence that the teacher has scaffolded students' written responses to text and that students are becoming increasingly more independent in developing quality answers to open-ended comprehension questions.	
There is evidence that the students understand what they are to do during independent-work time, including the tasks they must complete.	
The teacher selects independent activities that are clearly connected to the curriculum and are not just "busy work."	
The teacher provides a reasonable number of follow-up activities—not so many that students are overwhelmed, but enough to keep them focused on literacy for the duration of the time.	

PROTOCOL FOR REFLECTING ON A MODEL LESSON

Model lesson presented by: _____

Model lesson observed by: _____

Date of the lesson: _____

Lesson objective: _____

1. What did you notice? (Identify at least three specific observations, key moments in the teaching and learning.)

2. Was the objective met? What is the evidence? (State in terms of student performance.)

3. What do you think accounts for the success/lack of success? (Look for specifics.)

4. Is there something that you saw today that you'd like to try in your own teaching of a similar lesson?

PROTOCOL FOR TEACHER SELF-REFLECTION

Teacher: _____   **Date:** _____

1. What did you do?

2. How did it go? What is the evidence?

3. Why did it go that way?

4. What might you do differently (or be sure to do the same way) in anothersimilar lesson?

5. Where will you go next with your instruction?

Incorporating Administrators' Support

- Protocol for Reflecting on Coaching
- Protocol for Administrator's Monitoring

The **Coaching Plan of Action** maps the journey that the coach and teacher will take together to move teaching and learning forward. It builds in accountability for the teacher. But what about the coach's accountability? The **Protocol for Reflecting on Coaching** provides a framework for conversation between a coach and an administrator, or a coach and an outside consultant, to sit down and reflect systematically on the coach's progress to date. The final support form, **Protocol for Administrator's Monitoring**, keeps the plan of action alive even after the coach has moved on through periodic monitoring of a teacher's improved professional practices by the building principal.

PROTOCOL FOR REFLECTING ON COACHING

Too many important conversations in schools are not "conversations" at all but hurried verbal exchanges between harried educators passing each other in the hall. Coaching is serious work and deserves a serious conversation. The **Protocol for Reflecting on Coaching** offers some guidelines for a coach and an administrator, or a coach and an outside consultant, to take a break from the action to thoughtfully consider "how is it going?" Sometimes busy principals with a dozen (at least) initiatives in their school don't know where to begin to sort out the complexities of what a coach does day to day and whether the coaching is achieving its intended outcomes. This protocol asks questions that can help to identify whether the coaching is on track: Where did we start, where are we now, and where are we going?

PROTOCOL FOR ADMINISTRATOR'S MONITORING

The **Protocol for Administrator's Monitoring** is a simple way to track instruction in classrooms where coaching has taken place. Once teachers have been coached in the improvement of an instructional literacy practice, do they *implement* it on a consistent basis? Because teachers are ultimately accountable to their administrator, not their literacy coach, this is a great form for coaches to provide to their principal. Using this protocol does not require a lengthy classroom visit or a thorough analysis of the quality of the instructional practice. It just asks for a quick classroom check to see if the teacher is doing what he and the coach have worked together to improve. For example, is small group instruction taking place each morning during the designated hour? Are students engaged in authentic independent-practice activities rather than packets of comprehension questions? Is the objective for the day posted for students to see? In buildings where administrators regularly monitor teachers' implementation of coached practices, there is more consistent teacher follow-through.

PROTOCOL FOR REFLECTING ON COACHING

Coach: _____   School: _____

Consultant/Administrator: _____   Date: _____

****

Identified needs:

Coaching interventions to date:

Successes:

Continuing challenges:

Current focus of work:

Support needed:

Next step(s):

Date of next meeting:

PROTOCOL FOR ADMINISTRATOR'S MONITORING

Teacher: _____ Administrator: _____

Date	Time	Expectation	Met	Not met	Comments

A Few Final Words

Coaching is not linear. You don't start at the beginning and move neatly on a straight path until you come to the finish line. Coaching is messy—two steps forward, one step back. You begin by examining a teacher's practice, followed by some modeling, followed by some co-teaching, followed by a return the same teacher to analyze his practice once more. You travel in a circle. Has there been a change for the better? If so, you can support another need for this teacher, or move to a different teacher. How will *you* decide where to start?

STUDY QUESTIONS FOR CHAPTER SEVEN

1. What principles guide the selection of teachers to coach in your building? Do you coach *all* teachers? The teachers who want to be coached? The teachers who need coaching most? Do you feel this is the best approach? What changes would you make?

2. How do *you* initiate the coaching process with a particular teacher in order to get the teacher "on board?" Do you have any thoughts on this to share with your coaching colleagues?

3. When you have coached a teacher and s/he knows what to do but chooses not to do it—then what? How do you handle such a situation?

4. What kind of support would be most beneficial from an administrator as you coach teachers? (I would be so grateful if my administrator would…)

5. What protocols provided at the end of this chapter can you use right now to guide your coaching process? How do you envision using each one?

6. Are there any other protocols you could design to serve additional coaching needs? Explain.

Applying What You Know

The Teaching Scenarios and How to Use Them

This chapter contains three teaching scenarios for you to analyze in which teachers are providing literacy instruction to their students. The first two scenarios, "Wondering about Good Instruction" and "A Morning in Ms. C.'s Classroom," show teachers and students working through an entire literacy block from shared (whole-class) instruction to reflection at the end of the morning. "Small-Group Instruction in Mr. Sayre's Fifth Grade" looks only at the "reinforcing knowledge" portion of the literacy block, focusing mostly on guided practice with a few insights into independent practice.

As you read each scenario, pause at the designated stopping points to respond to questions about the strengths and weaknesses in that portion of the instruction. I generally recommend using the **Protocol for Monitoring Instruction that Gradually Releases Responsibility to Students** (page 113) to reflect systematically on the quality of the teaching. You could also use the **Protocol for Coach's Observation and Conferring** (page 114) if your intent is primarily to consider coaching interventions. Both of these forms are found in **Chapter Seven**.

It is ideal to discuss your analysis of these scenarios with a group of colleagues—coaches, teachers, or administrators. To guide your reading and discussion, the study questions for this chapter are listed at the beginning of the chapter rather than the end, before the scenarios. Consider these general questions to move your thinking about each scenario from analysis to action.

An analysis of the strengths and weaknesses of each of the teaching scenarios that follow may be found on the Maupin House website at www.maupinhouse.com/boylesanalyses.php. As you reflect on each scenario, you may uncover components of the lesson not addressed in the published online analysis that you think are also noteworthy. In that case, send your lesson feedback to me (Nancy Boyles) via the website. Your analysis could be added to those currently provided so that other coaches may benefit from your insights.

1. What do you consider the strongest features of this teacher's instruction?

2. What do you consider the most significant weaknesses?

3. How would you initiate a conversation with this teacher after this lesson?

4. Does this teacher need a coaching plan? If so, use the **Coaching Plan of Action** to plan your work together.

5. In what ways will the coach need to support this teacher?

6. How can the administrator support this teacher?

7. What changes in literacy instruction will be expected of this classroom teacher?

8. What protocols might be useful for continued work with this teacher?

9. What next step will you suggest to start your work together?

10. How will you proceed if the teacher is resistant or does not make an effort to meet the identified expectations?

Scenario One: Wondering about Good Instruction in a Second-Grade Classroom

The scene is a second-grade classroom in a large city, though it could be a classroom of any grade level, anywhere. This classroom looks exceptionally inviting with spaces for children to work alone and as a large group. There's a cozy book nook where kids can read, complete with beanbag chairs, an area rug, shelves of stories attractively arranged at the students' eye level, and even a table lamp for extra ambience. The bulletin boards contain examples of students' work, authentic reading-writing tasks—none of those teacher-store cardboard cutouts here.

The children, about twenty-five in all, are gathered on the rug in the meeting area. The teacher sits facing them. A picture book lies on her lap as she quietly asks for everyone's attention. She doesn't have to ask twice. "Today I'm going to read you a story," she begins. (It was a fable, though not one that I recognized.)

1. What do you think of this classroom so far? Would you want your own child in this classroom? Explain.

"I'm going to show you how good readers ask questions as they read. You'll hear me stop at different points in this story and think out loud about the questions I am wondering about as I read. Is everyone ready to be a good listener?"

They are. The teacher does exactly as promised; she reads a page or two, stops, and shares the question inspired by that segment of text: "Here's a place where I have a question," she reflects. "I'm wondering what the mother bear will do next?" She reads another page, stops to share a question, then reads a bit more, stops to share another question. And so it goes.

Children begin to raise their hands now, eager to contribute their own thinking: "I have a question," offers a cutie with braids in the front row.

"No, no," the teacher advises. "It's *my* turn to be a good thinker; you'll have *your* turn in a few minutes. Right now, your job is to be a good listener." She returns to her reading and resumes thinking aloud about questions inspired by the text. There are no answers that follow these questions, simply more questions. At the end of the story, the teacher notes that she has, in fact, discovered the answers to several of the questions she asked. By this time the group has been sitting quietly (if not completely attentively) for about fifteen minutes, and the teacher recognizes that it would be a good idea to change venues.

2. What phases of instruction is the teacher addressing here? What is strong/weak about this portion of the lesson? How do you think this teaching will impact student performance later on? What would you have done differently here to lead to stronger student outcomes?

"Here's what we're going to do," she announces. "We're going to read in pairs. I've already made up the pairs and selected a book for you to read with your partner. I'm going to give you some sticky notes, and I want you to stop while you're reading when a question pops into your mind and jot that question on a sticky note."

In a mostly orderly manner, pairs of children and books march off to various classroom corners to do their reading. I wait and watch for a moment or two, then shoe-horn my way into a tight space behind a bookcase where two little boys are reading *Twinnies* (Harcourt, 1997), a picture book by Eve Bunting.

The first reader begins. "Last June I got twin baby sitters [sisters]. The w-wuh-wuh-where...what's that word?" he inquires.

"Worst," I offer, sweeping my finger across the word from left to right, hoping my new friend will focus on the visual cues.

"The worst that [thing] is that three [there] are two of them."

The first reader moves the book closer to his partner so he can have a go at the next page. The partner, preoccupied with distractions from elsewhere in the room, focuses his gaze toward the book, stumbles through the first sentence, and declares, "You read it; I don't know the words."

Child one doesn't miss a beat, though he does miss several words on the next page or two. I am tempted to intercede and remind the boys that they are overlooking the primary goal of the activity: to note questions and record them on the sticky notes. I restrain myself, wondering if and when they will turn their attention to this task.

And then they do, though I can't quite figure out the rationale for halting at this particular point. The reader suddenly declares, "We need to ask a question." Both boys study the page in front of them. "Why is the girl holding the baby's hand?" This question, I expect, is derived from the illustration as there is no mention of hand-holding in the text, itself. (Reading the text, however, may have offered an answer to this question.) After a number of erasures, the question is neatly (if not accurately) penned on the sticky note and affixed to the page. I think a couple of additional questions, also fairly obscure details, receive mention before the teacher calls the group back to the meeting area.

I have moved on by then to another partnership, two girls, who are engrossed in one of the *Amelia Bedelia* ("Emily Bed-a-whatever") stories through which they demonstrate similar strategy application.

3. Think about the explicit model of instruction. Did the teacher omit any steps before reaching this point in the lesson? How did it contribute to students' performance? Explain why the students' behavior was predictable based on the instruction they received.

Meanwhile, back on the rug, children are eager to share the questions they have created. The "hand-holding" inquiry seems as appropriate as others described, and receives hearty approval from the teacher. All children are congratulated for their use of "good reader" strategies before the session comes to an end.

4. What was the teacher attempting to do as she closed the lesson? Did this portion of the lesson succeed? Why or why not? What could the teacher have done differently?

5. Describe this lesson as you might have taught it. Include all of the appropriate steps of the **Model of Explicit Instruction (Gradual Release of Responsibility)**.

Scenario Two: A Morning in Ms. C.'s Fourth Grade

Ms. Corbin called all twenty-two fourth graders to the rug. There was the usual scuffling of chairs and feet as everyone made their way to the carpeted corner of the room that doubled as the classroom library. Books in bins filled the shelves that divided this area from the rest of the room. Two girls arrived at the orange beanbag chair at the same time and simultaneously made a dive for it. A knowing look from Ms. C. settled the issue without words. The little miss with the purple sweater plopped into the chair. Her friend quickly found a seat nearby.

1. What indicators do you note here regarding the classroom environment and classroom management?

All eyes appeared to be fixed on their teacher who had settled into the old wooden rocker in the corner of the meeting area. But in fact, it was the bag in the teacher's hand that held everyone's attention. "Guess what's in the Treasure Bag today," Ms. C. began. The bag itself was nothing special, just an old plastic bag with a drawstring, the kind that might once have held a box of shoes purchased at the mall. You couldn't see through it.

"Here, feel what's inside, Thomas." Ms. C. held the bag in front of a frail lad wearing a too-large sweatshirt. Thomas gripped the bag with both hands and explored it with his fingers.

"It's soft... and kind of squishy," he announced hesitantly. "Maybe it's a stuffed animal?" His response was more of a question than an answer. Eyes darted here and there to uncover possible clues about the identity of this week's book. Ms. C. called on Max. His eyes were glued to the words in green marker she'd scrawled on the white board.

He grabbed the bag and pondered it for a few seconds. "Just what I thought," he mused. He felt the bag one more time to confirm his hypothesis. "It's a stuffed spider." This, he announced with absolute certainty.

"And what makes you think it's a spider, Max?" Ms. C. prodded.

"I'm one-hundred-percent positive it's a spider because you wrote 'Amazing Arachnids' on the board and 'arachnid' is another word for spider."

"Let's see if Max is right. Sarah, open the bag and take out what's inside." The teacher handed the bag to Sarah. She reached in and pulled out...a friendly looking, black, stuffed spider, complete with eight bendable legs and two roving googly eyes.

---

2. What component of explicit instruction is the teacher addressing here? How is the lesson going so far? Why?

"Are we reading a book about spiders this week?" someone wanted to know.

"We are." Ms. C. got up from her chair and navigated delicately between the bodies on the rug to reach the white board in the front of the meeting area. She picked up the marker and wrote, "What we know about spiders," recording about a minute's worth of ideas as children offered them. Max reprised the fact that arachnids are spiders. Maria offered that spiders were insects (which no one challenged). Rhonda declared that spiders were "scary"—which would have set off a prolonged debate if Ms. C. hadn't squelched the point-counterpoint by suggesting that "scary" might be considered a personal opinion rather than a fact. She wanted to get on with the lesson itself.

3. What do you observe about the teaching now? What are the strengths in this part of the instruction? Is there anything you would have done differently?

She held up the book they would read as a shared experience. The title was exactly as Max had predicted: *Amazing Arachnids*. "Fiction or nonfiction?" she asked.

"Nonfiction," everyone responded in unison.

"What do we expect to find in nonfiction that can help us with our comprehension?"

"Table of contents...highlighted vocabulary words... photographs with captions... charts and graphs...glossary... " It was clear that these kids had had plenty of experience with informational text.

"Do we know the author Lucy Floyd?" Silence followed this question. "You're right. We probably don't know this author, so we can't count on that to help us this time. But I bet you'll know the answer to my next question: What do you think we'll learn from this book?"

It is nonfiction, so I bet we will learn important things about spiders," Amanda declared.

4. What did these fourth graders know about pre-reading strategies? How do you think Ms. C. established these routines?

"How will we know if the information is *important?*" Ms. C. pressed on, inviting Amanda to elaborate on her response.

She was thoughtful for a moment before suggesting, "If it is something about what spiders look like or how they survive or different kinds of spiders...those things could be important. You would want to remember the information for a really long time." Amanda sat back, satisfied with her very thorough response.

"Let's make a list of things that could be important about spiders—or any animal." Ms. C. grabbed a dry-erase marker and headed for the white board. Ideas quickly emerged:

Important Information about Animals

1. What does the animal look like?
2. Where does the animal live?
3. What does the animal eat?
4. Are there different kinds of this animal?
5. How does this animal protect himself?
6. Is this animal endangered?

Ms. C. was now ready to set the target. "So today let's agree that our target will be to notice things about spiders that are important, facts that we will want to remember for a really long time." She reached for the chart with the picture of a target and wrote on the line beneath the bull's eye.

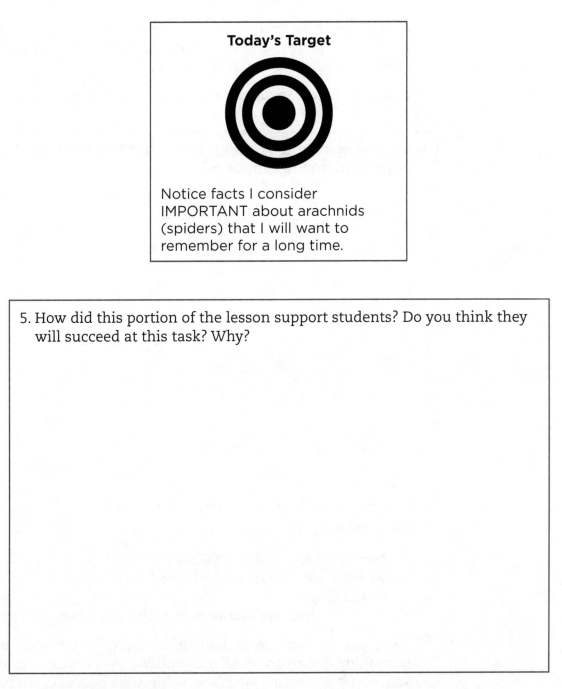

Today's Target

Notice facts I consider IMPORTANT about arachnids (spiders) that I will want to remember for a long time.

5. How did this portion of the lesson support students? Do you think they will succeed at this task? Why?

"Remember that the scientific name for spiders is 'arachnids'," Ms. C. reiterated as she passed out books to everyone. Another important word you'll see right on the first page is 'antennae.' What do you think that means?" "What other animals have antennae?" "Who can use the word 'antennae' in a sentence?" By the time she had clarified the definition and two or three students had supplied good sentences with the new word, she was back in her rocker with her own book in her hand.

"I'm going to read this first page out loud while you follow along. Every time we come to the word 'arachnid' or 'spider,' I'm going to stop reading, and all of you will read that word. I'll also stop when I notice something that I think is really important—and I'll think aloud about why I think it is so important. And one more thing: Why do you think I'm doing this thinking out loud?"

Everyone knew: "So we can do this later on our own," they chorused.

---

6. What do you notice about the instruction here? How is Ms. C. releasing responsibility to her students?

Ms. C. read the first paragraph:

> Take a close look at this little creature.
> At first glance it looks like an insect—but it's not.
> It's a wolf spider.
> **Amazing Arachnids** by Lucy Floyd (Celebration Press, 2002)

Ms. C. paused and looked thoughtful: "Okay, I'm already noticing something that might qualify as important—because it challenges something we *thought* we knew: Spiders are not really insects. That is definitely worth remembering because I think it's a common misunderstanding."

Ms. C. read on, pausing to note information about the number of different kinds of spiders that exist and where spiders make their home. She looked up when she'd reached the end of the second page. "Someone review for all of us how I identified information that I thought was *important* and worth remembering." Satisfied with the responses she received, she was ready to begin the next page. "But this time I'll be waiting to see how many of *you* can find some *important* facts about arachnids. Raise your hand when you think you hear one. And be prepared to tell me *why* you think it's important.

Hands shot up all round as the teacher read. "Go back and find the exact sentence with evidence of that fact," she requested as students shared their thinking. "Prove it in the text!" had become something of a classroom mantra, and these students hit that target every time. By the end of the first chapter (4 pages), the classroom clock (and a few wiggly kids) signaled that twenty minutes on the rug had been long enough.

7. What did you notice here about Ms. C.'s think-aloud? How did she bridge to more student responsibility?

Ms. C. stood up and began directing students to various corners of the room: "When you go back to your seats today, choose a nonfiction book that is "just right" for you. Remember the "five-finger rule" and think about other points on our "Just-Right Book" chart that make your book choice a good selection for you." She pointed to the directions she had printed on the board: "In your book, find at least three pieces of information that you consider *important* about your topic. Mark those places with a sticky note, and be ready to tell the class why you thought each fact was important."

Then Ms. C. clarified what else students would do in the hour ahead (also noted on the board): "When you are finished with your independent reading, you may find a partner and practice reading a favorite paragraph from *Amazing Arachnids* aloud until you sound like a news reporter. Check the "Fluency Chart" in your reading folder to see how your fluency is coming along. If you finish both of those tasks, move on to your writing. Let's get those revisions finished today; I know you know what to do."

"Table three, you may make your book selections now. Ms. C. appraised the situation as students from each table in turn made their way to the library corner. Satisfied that everyone was on task, she called Mario, Sam, L'Quisha, Jarvon, and Anna to the reading table. "Let's work on this strategy together before you use it in your independent book," she began.

Fast forward one hour. The five students who stayed with Ms. C. initially were now back at their seats, replaced by six other children applying "the important" criteria to a text about Harriet Tubman that challenged their above-grade-level reading skills. Meanwhile, Ms. C. had popped up from her seat at the reading table a few times to circulate among students back at their desks as students at the table read silently: "How's it going, Micah? Show me where you're stuck, Michelle." Now she scanned the room one more time: "Okay, everybody, you have one minute to finish the sentence you're reading or writing right now. Then come back to the rug."

---

8. Reflect on the transition to "reinforcing knowledge." Was this effective? Why? You are not given too many details about the quality of Ms. C.'s small-group instruction. But what can you tell about it from the information provided?

They complied, amid a rustle of papers and books. "So who found something important?"

"We found lots of important stuff in our poem about Harriet Tubman," Alesha offered. She shared her discoveries, along with some insights about *why* each point seemed noteworthy.

"I found some important facts about the planets," Ryan announced, "like Mars is called the 'red planet.'"

"I don't think that's so important," Michael blurted out. "Everybody knows Mars is the 'red planet.'" Ms. C. was on the verge of chastising Michael for his lack of judgment in criticizing his classmate's contribution but decided there was, perhaps, a larger lesson to be learned here.

"Let's think about this," she began. "Will we all always think the same information is *important?*" An animated discussion followed in which students reached the conclusion that what a person finds noteworthy is based on your schema or background knowledge on a particular topic.

Ms. C. pressed on: "How could we be wrong about identifying information as 'important?'"

Michael was the first one with his hand up. "We could be wrong is if you couldn't prove it in the text."

Celia had an idea, too: "We could be wrong if it was just a little, tiny detail that didn't matter very much."

"Good," Ms. C. responded, although she didn't pursue this point now. She would tuck this observation away as a possible launching point for a follow-up lesson.

9. What did you think about this part of Ms. C.'s lesson? What did it accomplish? How can she use this information for future instruction?

Instead she asked, "If you were explaining to someone who had been absent today how to go about identifying important information in nonfiction text, what would you tell her?"

"I'd tell her to look for facts that answered some of those questions up there," Ryan offered, nodding toward the "Important Facts" chart the class had created prior to today's reading.

"Would that be a good *strategy* to use?" Ms. C. queried. "Would that be a good way to approach the reading?" Everyone thought that's what good readers should do.

"So based on what we worked on today, what do you think we should do tomorrow?" Ms. C. liked to ask this question at the end of a shared lesson.

"We could read the next chapter and find more important pieces of information about spiders," someone suggested.

"We could definitely do that," Ms. C. responded tentatively, hoping someone would think abut that final step in mastering those oh-so-important power standards.

Luis came to the rescue: "We should think about how we would write a good answer to a question about this."

"Sounds like a plan," Ms. C. concluded. "Tomorrow we'll think about how we can get our good thinking down on paper."

10. Do you think this was an important instructional step? Why or why not?

11. Think about the teacher types described in Chapter Six. Into which group would Ms. C. probably fit? How could a coach best support her?

Scenario Three: Small-Group Instruction in the Fifth Grade

Shared reading in Mr. Sayre's fifth grade was over for the day. The class was studying fairy tales from different cultures and this morning, Mr. S. had read *The Rough-Face Girl* (Scholastic, 1993) by Rafe Martin. The session concluded as it usually did with directions for students' morning work. They would create a Venn diagram comparing this Algonquin version of the *Cinderella* story to the more traditional tale with which they were familiar. They would also complete a sheet of ten comprehension questions to check their literal understanding of the story. Additionally, most students had an essay to finish that they had started yesterday in preparation for the state achievement test, which was now just a week away. The pressure was on to practice, practice, practice in order to improve on last year's dismal literacy scores. "When your other work is done, you may continue reading your independent book," Mr. S. reminded his students.

1. What do you think about Mr. Sayre's instruction so far? We don't know what occurred during shared reading, but what about the way he set up independent work time: Does it sound like this was a smooth transition? What about the independent tasks? Will they help his students move forward as readers and writers? Do students have enough to keep them busy for the next hour? What would you have done differently?

Mr. S. surveyed the classroom action for a couple of minutes, waiting for everyone to settle into their morning routine, then called a group of six students to the kidney-shaped table at the back of the room. This was one of four groups in Mr. Sayre's fifth grade and would be considered slightly below grade level by most standards. Mr. Sayre wished he could meet with these students every day but said that the best he could manage was three times a week, the same amount of time he spent with all his groups—the one group that was lower than this, as well as the two groups of more advanced readers. Actually, he didn't see his highest group more than twice during most weeks, he confessed.

Mr. S. distributed a paperback copy of the book, *Lon Po Po: A Red-Riding Hood Story from China* (Scholastic, 1989) by Ed Young, to each of his six students. The books looked brand new and students were immediately drawn to the illustration of the sinister-looking wolf against the bright red background of the cover. "What's the title?" he began. "What do you think the story is about?" A couple of children flipped the book over, presumably to consult the blurb on the back, but there was none. "Take a picture walk," the teacher prompted. "Make some predictions about what you think will happen in this story."

---

2. What have you learned about Mr. S. now? Comment on the frequency with which he sees is groups. Did he begin his small-group instruction in an appropriate way? What do these students know about reading? Would you have approached this text differently? Explain.

Several minutes ticked by as students lost themselves in the beautiful images on each page. It was hard to tell whether they were making the requested predictions, or if they were simply mesmerized by the menacing wolf and the frightened faces of the three little girls peering out from the swirl of color on each page.

"I think this version of the story has three girls in it and the wolf ends up in a tree," Alisa offered.

"Who is Lon Po Po?" Raymond wondered aloud.

"On the first page it looks like it's the *mother* who is leaving with the basket. That's way different than the story we know where Red Riding Hood takes the basket to Granny's house," Dominic suggested.

"The pictures look Chinese," Leah commented.

Mr. Sayre acknowledged each response, though he didn't expand on any of them. He did use Leah's observation about the "Chinese pictures" to ask the students if they knew where China was. Everyone seemed to know it was in Asia, especially Leah who had been adopted from China as a baby.

---

3. What was accomplished during this portion of the instruction? How would you have supported this part of the reading process?

Mr. S. looked at his watch and charged forward, producing a short stack of vocabulary cards, each word typed on a piece of paper about 1 x 3 inches. "Let's look at these," he instructed, nodding toward the first term: *gingko nuts*. When no one could tell him what *ginkgo nuts* were, he grabbed the dictionary from the shelf behind him and read the definition aloud. A similar introduction followed with ten other words: *eldest, disguised, latched, cunning, plump, hemp, clever, brittle, pluck, fetched*.

Discussion of these words (dominated by teacher talk) was punctuated by reminders to children at their seats to "follow class rules." Mr. S. interrupted his small-group instruction three times to refocus students whose off-task behavior was distracting their classmates: "We sharpen our pencils before school, Lucas... Margaret, why are you out of your seat again?... Jevon, what did I say to do when your work was finished?"

4. In this section you observed more about Mr. S's pre-reading strategies as well as his classroom management. Comment on both. What did you like/not like about his vocabulary instruction? Could the management issues have been avoided?

"Where does the time go?" Mr. S. sighed to the students seated at the reading table. "Take *Lon Po Po* back to your seats and read the first half of the story." He showed the students where to stop since the pages were unnumbered. "Next time we meet we will talk about what has happened in the book so far."

The students were quickly dismissed back to their seats. This group had taken half an hour rather than the intended twenty minutes. It looked like Mr. S. would only get to two of his groups again this morning! He quickly called his second group, his lowest readers, to the table. They brought with them copies of *The Gingerbread Boy* (Harper, 2000) by Richard Egielski that they had begun reading two days ago, the last time they met.

5. Now you have seen the entire lesson. What was strong/weak in this final portion? If this lesson was similar to others that Mr. S. teaches, what do you anticipate about the literacy growth of his students?

6. If you had twenty minutes to work with this group, how would you have organized your time? Explain what you would have included in this lesson and how many minutes you would have spent on each component.

Bibliography of Professional Resources

The books listed below are resources that coaches might wish to access to increase their own knowledge about literacy research and best practices or to support teachers in their building in need of professional insights into various areas of reading and writing. Of course, there are other resources available: journal articles, websites, videos, and DVDs. New books are published every day! There are also additional subtopics related to literacy that could be identified. Think of the list here as a sample to get you started.

Literacy Research and Practice: Differentiated Instruction and Multiple Dimensions

Allington, R. L. & Cunningham, P. M. (2002). *Schools That Work: Where All Children Read and Write (2nd ed.)*. Boston: Allyn & Bacon.

Barone, D., Hardman, D., & Taylor, J. (2004). *Reading First in the Classroom*. Boston: Allyn & Bacon.

Clifford, T. (2006). *The Middle School Writing Toolkit: Differentiated Instruction across the Content Areas*. Gainesville, FL: Maupin House.

Cummins, C., Ed. (2006). *Understanding and Implementing Reading First Initiatives: The Changing Role of Administrators*. Newark, DE: International Reading Association.

Duffy, G. G. (2003). *Explaining Reading: A Resource for Teaching Concepts, Skills, andStrategies*. New York: The Guilford Press.

Ellery, V. (2005). *Creating Strategic Readers: Techniques for Developing Competency in Phonemic Awareness, Phonics, Fluency, Vocabulary, and Comprehension*. Newark, DE: International Reading Association.

Flippo, R. F. (2003). *Assessing Readers: Qualitative Diagnosis and Instruction*. Portsmouth, NH: Heinemann.

Hoyt, L. (2000). *Snapshots: Literacy Minilessons up Close*. Portsmouth, NH: Heinemann. International Reading Association. (2000). *Making a Difference means making It Different: Honoring Children's Rights to Excellent Reading Instruction* (Position statement).

Newark, DE: International Reading Association. National Institute of Child Health and Human Development. (2000). *Report of the National Reading Panel. Teaching Children to Read: An Evidence-Based Assessment of the Scientific Research Literature on Reading and Its Implications for Reading Instruction* (NIH Publication No. 00-4769). Washington, D.C.: U.S. Government Printing Office.

Pressley, M. (2005). *Reading Instruction That Works: The Case for Balanced Teaching (3rd Ed.).* New York: The Guilford Press.

Robinson, R. D., McKenna, M. C., & Wedman, J. M., Eds. (2000). *Issues and Trends in Literacy Education (2nd ed.).* Boston: Allyn & Bacon.

Walpole, S. & McKenna, M. C. (2007). *Differentiated Reading Instruction: Strategies for the Primary Grades.* New York: The Guilford Press.

Phonemic Awareness, Phonics, and Spelling

Adams, M. J. (1990). *Beginning to Read: Thinking and Learning about Print.* Cambridge, MA: MIT Press.

Adams, M. J., Beeler, T., Foorman, B. R., Lundberg, I. (1997). *Phonemic Awareness in Young Children: A Classroom Curriculum.* Baltimore: Brookes Publishing Company.

Bear, D. R., Invernizzi, M., Templeton, S., & Johnston, F. (1999). *Words Their Way: Word Study for Phonics, Vocabulary, and Spelling Instruction.* Upper Saddle River, NJ: Merrill.

Blevins, W. (1999). *Phonics from A to Z: A Practical guide.* New York: Scholastic.

Blevins, W. (2001). *Teaching Phonics & Word Study in the Intermediate Grades.* New York: Scholastic.

Cunningham, P. M., Hall, D. P, & Heggie, T. (2001). *Making Words: Multilevel, Hands-On, Developmentally Appropriate Spelling and Phonics Activities.* Torrance, CA: Good Apple. (Other books in this series, too)

Cunningham, P. M. (2000). *Phonics They Use: Words for Reading and Writing.* New York: Longman.

Ericson, L., & Juliebo, M. F. (1998). *The Phonological Awareness Handbook for Kindergarten and Primary Teachers.* Newark, DE: International Reading Association.

Ganske, K. (2000). *Word Journeys: Assessment-Guided Phonics, Spelling, and Vocabulary Instruction.* New York: The Guilford Press.

McCormick, C. E., Throneburg, R. N., & Smitley, J. M. (2002). *A Sound Start: Phonemic Awareness Lessons for Reading Success.* New York: The Guilford Press.

Mitten, L.K. (2005). *20-in-10: Linking Music and Literacy with Twenty, Ten-Minute Mini-Lessons and Activities for Primary Learners.* Gainesville, FL: Maupin House.

Opitz, M.F. (2000). *Rhymes & Reasons: Literature and Language Play for Phonological Awareness.* Portsmouth, NH: Heinemann.

Zgonc, Y. (2000). *Sounds in Action: Phonological Awareness Activities & Assessment.* Peterborough, NH: Crystal Springs Books.

Vocabulary Instruction

Beck, I. L., McKeown, M. G., & Kucan, L. (2002). *Bringing Words to Life: Robust Vocabulary Instruction.* New York: The Guilford Press. (Also good for oral language)

Blachowicz, C., & Fisher, P.J. (2001). *Teaching Vocabulary in All Classrooms (2nd Ed.).* Upper Saddle River, NJ: Merrill/Prentice Hall.

Brassell, D. & Flood, J. (2003). *Vocabulary Strategies Every Teacher Needs to Know.* San Diego, CA: Academic Professional Development.

Johnson, D. D. (2000). *Vocabulary in the Elementary and Middle School.* Boston: Allyn & Bacon.

Ohanian, S. (2002). *The Great Word Catalogue: Fundamental Activities for Building Vocabulary.* Portsmouth, NH: Heinemann.

Fluency

Black, A., & Stave, A. (2007). *A Comprehensive Guide to Readers Theatre: Enhancing Fluency and Comprehension in Middle School and Beyond.* Newark, DE: International Reading Association.

Brand, M. & Brand, G. (2006). *Practical Fluency: Classroom Perspectives, Grades K-6.* Portland, ME: Stenhouse.

Johns, J. L, & Berglund, R. L. (2006). *Fluency: Strategies & Assessments, Third Edition.* Dubuque, IA: Kendall/Hunt.

Rasinski, T. V. (2003). *The Fluent Reader: Oral Reading Strategies for Building Word*

Recognition, Fluency, and Comprehension. New York: Scholastic.

Rasinski, T.V., & Padak, N. (2005). *3-Minute Reading Assessments: Word Recognition, Fluency, and Comprehension (Grades 1-4).* New York: Scholastic.

Rasknski, T. V., & Padak, N. (2005). *3-Minute Reading Assessments: Word Recognition, Fluency, and Comprehension (Grades 5-8).* New York: Scholastic.

Samuels, S. J. & Farstrup, A. E., Eds. (2006). *What Research Has to Say about Fluency Instruction.* Newark, DE: International Reading Association.

Comprehension

Allen, J. (2000). *Yellow Brick Roads: Shared and Guided Paths to Independent Reading 4-12.* Portland, ME: Stenhouse.

Blachowicz, C. & Ogle, D. (2001). *Reading Comprehension: Strategies for Independent Learners.* New York: The Guilford Press.

Block, C. C., Rodgers, L. L. & Johnson, R. B. (2004). *Comprehension Process Instruction: Creating Reading Success in Grades K-3.* New York: The Guilford Press.

Block, C. C., & Pressley, M., Eds. (2001). *Comprehension Instruction: Research-Based Best Practices.* New York: The Guilford Press.

Boyles, N. N. (2001). *Teaching Written Response to Text: Constructing Quality Answers to Open-Ended Comprehension Questions.* Gainesville, FL: Maupin House.

Boyles, N. N. (2004). *Constructing Meaning through Kid-Friendly Comprehension Strategy Instruction.* Gainesville, FL: Maupin House.

Harvey, S., & Goudvis, A. (2007). *Strategies That Work: Teaching Comprehension for Understanding and Engagement (2nd Ed.).* Portland, ME: Stenhouse.

Hoyt, L. (1998). *Revisit, Reflect, Retell: Strategies for Improving Reading Comprehension.* Portsmouth, NH: Heinemann.

Keene, E. O., & Zimmermann, S. (2007). *Mosaic of Thought: The Power of Comprehension Strategy Instruction (2nd Ed.).* Portsmouth, NH: Heinemann.

Miller, D. (2002). *Reading with Meaning: Teaching Comprehension in the Primary Grades.* Portland, ME: Stenhouse.

Roser, N. L., & Martinez, M. G., Eds. (2005). *What a Character! Character Study as a Guide to Literary Meaning Making in Grades K-8.* Newark, DE: International Reading Association.

Tovani, C. (2000). *I Read It, but I Don't Get It: Comprehension Strategies for Adolescent Readers.* Portland, ME: Stenhouse.

Oral Language

Benson, V., & Cummins, C. (2000). *The Power of Retelling: Developmental Steps for Building Comprehension.* Bothell, WA: Wright Group/McGraw-Hill.

Johnston, P. H. (2004). *Choice Words: How Our Language Affects Children's Learning.* Portland, ME: Stenhouse.

Optitz, M. F., & Rasinski, T. V. (1998). *Good-Bye Round Robin: 25 Effective Oral Reading Strategies.* Portsmouth, NH: Heinemann.

Roskos, K. A., Tabors, P. O., & Lenhart, L. A. (2004). *Oral Language and Early Literacy in Preschool: Talking, Reading, and Writing.* Newark, DE: International Reading Association.

Trelease, J. (1995). *The Read-Aloud Handbook (4th Ed.).* New York: Penguin.

Writing

Anderson, C. (2005). *Assessing Writers.* Portsmouth, NH: Heinemann.

Anderson, C. (2000). *How's It Going: A Practical Guide to Conferring with Student Writers.* Portsmouth, NH: Heinemann.

Culham, R. (2005). *6 + 1 Traits of Writing: The Complete Guide for the Primary Grades.* New York: Scholastic.

Culham, R. (2003). *6 + 1 Traits of Writing: The Complete Guide (Grades 3 and Up).* New York: Scholastic.

Fletcher, R. & Portalupi, J. (1998). *Craft Lessons: Teaching Writing K-8.* Portland, ME: Stenhouse.

Fletcher, R. (1992). *What a Writer Needs.* Portsmouth, NH: Heinemann.

Forney, M. (2005). *Primary Pizzazz Writing.* Gainesville, FL: Maupin House.

Freeman, M. S. (1998). *Teaching the Youngest Writers: A Practical Guide.* Gainesville, FL: Maupin House.

Graham, S., MacArthur. C. A., & Fitzgerald, J. (2007). *Best Practices in Writing Instruction.* New York: The Guilford Press.

Lane, B. (1993). *After the End: Teaching and Learning Creative Revision.* Portsmouth, NH: Heinemann.

Ray, K. W. (1999). *Wondrous Words: Writers and Writing in the Elementary Classroom.* Urbana, IL: National Council of Teachers of English.

Rog, L. J. (2007). *Marvelous Minilessons for Teaching Beginning Writing, K-3.* Newark, DE: International Reading Association.

Schrecengost, M. (2001). *Writing Whizardry: 60 Mini-Lessons to Teach Elaboration & Writer's Craft.* Gainesville, FL: Maupin House.

Spandel, V. (2004). *Creating Writers through 6-Trait Writing Assessment and Instruction, (4th Ed.).* Boston: Allyn & Bacon.

Spandel, V. (2003). *Creating Young Writers: Using the Six Traits to Enrich Writing Process in Primary Classrooms.* New York: Pearson.

Motivation

Brophy, J. (2004). *Motivating Students to Learn (2nd Ed.).* Mahwah, NJ: Lawrence Erlbaum Associates.

Pressley, M., Dolezal, S. E., Raphael, L. M., Mohan, L., Roehrig, A. D., & Bogner, K. (2003). *Motivating Primary-Grade Students*. New York: The Guilford Press.

Verhoeven, L. & Snow, C., Eds. (2001). *Literacy and Motivation: Reading Engagement in Individuals and Groups*. Mahwah, NJ: Lawrence Erlbaum Associates.

Small-Group/Guided Instruction

Caldwell, J. S. & Ford, M. P. (2002). *Where Have All the Bluebirds Gone? How to Soar with Flexible Grouping*. Portsmouth, NH: Heinemann.

Diller, D. (2007). *Making the Most of Small Groups: Differentiation for All*. Portland, ME: Stenhouse.

McLaughlin, M. & Allen, M. B. (2002). *Guided Comprehension: A Teaching Model for Grades 3-8*. Newark, DE: International Reading Association.

McLaughlin, M. (2003). *Guided Comprehension in the Primary Grades*. Newark, DE: International Reading Association.

Tyner, B. (2003). *Small-Group Reading Instruction: A Differentiated Teaching Model for Beginning and Struggling Readers*. Newark, DE: International Reading Association.

Tyner, B., & Green, S. E. (2005). *Small-Group Reading Instruction: A Differentiated Teaching Model for Intermediate Readers, Grades 3-8*. Newark, DE: International Reading Association.

Reading Nonfiction

Duke, N. K. & Bennett-Armistead, V. S. (2003). *Reading & Writing Informational Text in the Primary Grades: Research-Based Practices*. New York: Scholastic.

Hoyt, L. (2002). *Make It Real: Strategies for Success with Informational Texts*. Portsmouth, NH: Heinemann.

Hoyt, L., Mooney, M., & Parkes, B. (2003). *Exploring Informational Texts: From Theory to Practice*. Portsmouth, NH: Heinemann.

Kletzien, S. B., & Dreher, M. J. (2003). *Informational Text in K-3 Classrooms: Helping Children Read and Write*. Newark, DE: International Reading Association.

Moss, B. (2003). *Exploring the Literature of Fact: Children's Nonfiction Trade Books in the Elementary Classroom*. New York: The Guilford Press.

Stead, T. (2005). *Reality Checks: Teaching Reading Comprehension with Nonfiction, K-5*. Portland, ME: Stenhouse.

Stead, T. (2001). *Is That a Fact? Teaching Nonfiction Writing K-3*. Portland, ME: Stenhouse.

English Language Learners

Ariza, E. W. (2005). *Not for ESOL Teachers: What Every Classroom Teacher Needs to Know about the Linguistically, Culturally, and Ethnically Diverse Student.* Boston: Allyn & Bacon.

Cary, S. (2000). *Working with Second Language Learners: Answers to Teachers' Top Ten Questions.* Portsmouth, NH: Heinemann.

Freeman, D. E., & Freeman Y. S. (2000). *Teaching Reading in Multilingual Classrooms.* Portsmouth, NH: Heinemann.

Hurley, S. R. & Tinajero, J. V. (2000). *Literacy Assessment of Second Language Learners.* Boston: Allyn & Bacon.

Young, T. A. & Hadaway, N. L. (2005). *Supporting the Literacy Development of English Learners: Increasing Success in All Classrooms.* Newark, DE: International Reading Association.

Interventions for Struggling Readers

Allington, R. L. (2001). *What Really Matters for Struggling Readers: Designing Research-Based Programs.* New York: Longman.

Beers, K. (2003). *When Kids Can't Read: What Teachers Can Do: A Guide for Teachers 6-12.* Portsmouth, NH: Heinemann.

Crawley, S. J. & Merritt, K. (2004). *Remediating Reading Difficulties (4th Ed.).* New York: McGraw Hill.

Fink, R. (2006). *Why Jane and John Couldn't Read—and How They Learned: A New Look at Striving Readers.* Newark, DE: International Reading Association.

Lyons, C. (2003). *Teaching Struggling Readers: How to Use Brain-Based Research to Maximize Learning.* Portsmouth, NH: Heinemann.

McKenna, M. C. (2002). *Help for Struggling Readers: Strategies for Grades 3-8.* New York: The Guilford Press.

Strickland, D. S., Ganske, K., & Monroe, J. K. (2001). *Supporting Struggling Readers and Writers: Strategies for Classroom Intervention 3-6.* Portland, ME: Stenhouse.

Wirt, B., Bryan, C. B., & Wesley, K. D. (2005). *Discovering What Works for Struggling Readers: Journeys of Exploration with Primary-Grade Students.* Newark, DE: International Reading Association.

Teaching literacy in an urban environment

Barone, D. M. (2006). *Narrowing the Literacy Gap: What Works in High-Poverty Schools.* New York: The Guilford Press.

Delpit, L. (1995). *Other People's Children: Cultural Conflict in the Classroom.* New York: The New Press.

Delpit, L. & Dowdy, J. K., Eds. (2002). *The Skin That We Speak: Thoughts on Language and Culture in the Classroom.* New York: The New Press.

Lapp, D., Block, C. C., Cooper, E. J., Flood, J., Roser, N., & Tinajero, J. (2004). *Teaching All the Children: Strategies for Developing Literacy in An Urban Setting.* New York: The Guilford Press.

Lazar, A.M. (2004). *Learning to Be Literacy Teachers in Urban Schools: Stories of Growth and Change.* Newark, DE: International Reading Association.

Mason, P. A. & Schumm, J. S., Eds. (2003). *Promising Practices for Urban Reading Instruction.* Newark, DE: International Reading Association.

Singleton, G. D. & Linton, C. (2005). *Courageous Conversations about Race: A Field Guide*

Notes

Notes

Notes

Notes

Notes